The Gifts They Bring

The Gifts They Bring

How Children in the Gospels Can Shape Inclusive Ministry

AMY LINDEMAN ALLEN

1st edition
Published by Westminster John Knox Press
Louisville, Kentucky

23 24 25 26 27 28 29 30 31 32—10 9 8 7 6 5 4 3 2 1

Book design by Sharon Adams
Cover design by Marc Whitaker / MTWdesign.net
Cover art by Mike Moyers. Used by permission.

Library of Congress Cataloging-in-Publication Data

Names: Allen, Amy Lindeman, author.
Title: The gifts they bring : how children in the gospels can shape inclusive ministry / Amy Lindeman Allen.
Description: 1st edition. | Louisville, Kentucky : Westminster John Knox Press, [2023] | Includes bibliographical references. | Summary: "Through a rereading of familiar Gospel accounts, Allen celebrates children as a gift to the church and offers insight on the many gifts children themselves bring to ministry today"— Provided by publisher.
Identifiers: LCCN 2023020923 (print) | LCCN 2023020924 (ebook) | ISBN 9780664268343 (paperback) | ISBN 9781646983384 (ebook)
Subjects: LCSH: Children in the Bible. | Children--Religious aspects--Christianity. | Bible. Gospels--Commentaries.
Classification: LCC BS576 .A45 2023 (print) | LCC BS576 (ebook) | DDC 226/.06--dc23/eng/20230701
LC record available at https://lccn.loc.gov/2023020923
LC ebook record available at https://lccn.loc.gov/2023020924

To

Roger and Joanne,
whose faithful love and inclusion of all God's children
is an inspiration and model for me.

"One generation shall laud your works to another, and shall declare your mighty acts."

—Psalm 145:4

Contents

Foreword

Amy Lindeman Allen is a biblical scholar, pastor, educator, and parent. Her experiences in all of these roles, as well as her talents and insights, are woven together in this book as she invites readers to think in new ways about beloved Gospel stories. Just as Jesus confronted those he met with their assumptions, so too we, as contemporary hearers today, can imagine new ways that children listen, share, participate, proclaim, advocate, and live in partnership with us in being God's faithful disciples at work in the world.

What story is your church telling? That is the question at the heart of this book. Each chapter offers you the opportunity to hear a contemporary story and then reflect on its meaning in light of a Gospel story. This seamless movement between ancient and contemporary stories invites you to consider the gifts that children bring when they are welcomed and supported in their participation and leadership in congregational life. The connection among these stories is made evident by the gifts that are nurtured and sustained when all ages are welcomed into the faith life of a congregation. As Allen reminds us, welcoming a child is welcoming Jesus. Is our welcome to children in worship contingent on how quiet and passive they are? Whose voice is heard and valued? Are opportunities for service and mission limited only to adults?

Author and theologian Phyllis Tickle once commented that the church should have a large rummage sale every 500 years to bring out all the stuff that has accumulated. Sort everything—theologies, practices, ways of interpreting Scripture—and decide what to keep, what to discard, and what to recycle. I think we are at the beginning of that church rummage sale. We sit on a cusp of possibility. Either we retreat into the past—"We've always done it this way" or "We've never done it that way"—or we imagine new ways we can intentionally be church together across the ages.

A hymn written by Marty Haugen in 1995 similarly invites us to imagine the house we build where all are welcome, where everyone is named, "taught and claimed as words within the Word."[1]

Seeing how some of his disciples attempted to block the parents and children coming to see him, Jesus opened his arms so they could participate in his loving welcome. Young shepherds proclaimed the good news of the birth of the child whose story we still tell. Jesus invited fishers to follow him, to live into the ways they could each be advocates for a life of inclusion for all who were hungry; thirsty; or needing clothing, shelter, or friends. Jesus noticed and listened. When he was at Martha's house, he saw how Mary was listening and learning and the ways that Martha was offering hospitality and welcome. Both were serving as his disciples. A child's lunch fed a crowd, and Jesus helped people see how God's realm is revealed in the sharing of bread. The healing of a distraught mother's son invites our consideration of the ways we can live together as partners in faithful communities wherever we live.

With her close and imaginative reading of these familiar biblical stories, Allen invites us to begin the rummage sale by considering the ways we invite and support faith in disciples of all ages—those with autism and neurodiverse abilities, those for whom hearing or vision is a challenge, those who wrestle with who they are and what they are called to be and do in this world, those who are quite sure of what they believe, those who come with many questions, and everyone in between. God's family is complete when the gifts of all are welcomed at the doors of the church.

The Gifts They Bring is a gift to the church. Read and discuss it together, and consider the story your church is telling about the ways the gifts of all are being invited, supported, and challenged for the ministry that God is calling forth in us. Together find new ways to tell old stories and share new gifts as you work to build a house that embodies God's Word.

Elizabeth F. Caldwell
McCormick Theological Seminary,
professor emerita, and author of
I Wonder: Engaging a Child's Curiosity about the Bible

Acknowledgments

This book is dedicated to my grandparents, Roger and Joanne. From my first childhood fancies to the discernment of my call to ministry, they never stopped believing in me and helping me to recognize the gifts that I can bring to the church and the world—even as my direction changed more than a few times along the way. When my academic dissertation was published, they were among the first to read it, through the academic jargon and literature reviews, even though they have no special interest in biblical criticism or theology. They graciously thanked me for gifting them a copy of that book but told me it would also be nice if, someday, I wrote a book that was easier to read and understand. They were the first to plant the seed in my head, and the hope that they might have the opportunity to read this book has been a continual inspiration along the journey of its development.

While my grandparents were the first to encourage me to write for the church, they were far from the last. Over the past several years I have had the opportunity to teach about children and the Bible in countless Christian education settings across the church, ranging from clergy and lay education events to adult forums to intergenerational seminars to preschool Sunday school classes. I have both learned from and been affirmed by the students in each of these sessions. Over and over again, as I point out children who are hiding just beneath the surface of many of our favorite biblical texts, or bring to life the perspective of those with whom we have become overly familiar, people have asked me if I have written about that. The curiosity and affirmations of each person who has been generous enough to engage with me about this topic have been a gift to me in my writing process, and this book is intended as a gift to them in turn.

At the same time, writing for a church audience is quite different from writing for academicians and seminarians and even from preaching and teaching in the church. It is a process that combines the best of both, but it is, at the same time, an altogether different labor entirely. Coming to this realization was a journey, and I am indebted to my editor, Jessica Miller Kelley, for accompanying me along the way. From the first inquiry I sent to her until the last edits before this book went to print, Jessica has steadfastly walked alongside me in the art of church writing, first helping me to clarify the gifts the children in these biblical texts bring to bear on today's church, and then offering questions and comments along the way that helped me to gain clarity in my thoughts without dismissing them. In so doing, she helped me to dig deeper into the meaning of these biblical stories not only for the first century, but for today. I am indebted to her wisdom and grace.

Likewise, my parents, Bonnie and Roland Lindeman, have been a support and a guide to me always; that has been true especially in this writing process. As a pastor who is gifted in preaching children's sermons, my father is a natural resource for ideas and perspectives, and I am grateful for his ear and guidance as I grow in my ministry. As a layperson, however, my mother was the most instrumental in helping me to shift my target audience from preachers to the people in the pews. Throughout the writing process, she read multiple drafts of each chapter and talked me through each one, at times line by line, noting what she found helpful and inspiring, what she wanted to know more about, and, even more helpfully, what she didn't understand or found to be too bogged down with detail. It is with thanks to both my parents that I hope this book will be beneficial to both pastors and laypeople alike.

Additionally, this book would not have been possible without the time and resources so graciously granted both by my institution and my family. The faculty and board of Christian Theological Seminary

(CTS) granted me a research leave in the fall of 2021. During that time I completed the bulk of the writing of this book. More importantly, collegial support of my work at the intersections of praxis and scholarship has given me both the freedom and the incentive to pursue this project. I'm especially grateful to the students who have participated in the Children and the Bible course I teach at CTS. The unique mix of students preparing for both counseling and pastoral ministries with whom I have had the privilege of working in each of these course sections has opened up these stories for me in ways I would not have imagined otherwise and confirmed the importance of attending to the gifts that children bring not just in the Bible, but for the church. And, of course, I am grateful to my spouse, Erik, and my children, Becca, Joanna, and William, who have offered encouragement and understanding, even when at times I had to pull late nights editing chapters or spend Sundays away from our worship homes, teaching in churches across our community. They have even generously allowed for parts of their own stories to be shared in this book. I could not get through this work, or this life, without them.

Finally, this book is the product of more than fifteen years of ministry among God's faithful people, and it rests on the shoulders of all of the people and churches with whom I have had the privilege of serving over that time. Our stories are interconnected, and I am indebted to each church and individual for letting me be a small part of theirs.

Introduction

A Child-Centered Approach to Scripture and Ministry

Our oldest child, Becca, received her first Holy Communion by mistake. Actually, it wasn't so much a mistake as it was an intuitive act of inclusion. It was a blessing of the best sort, but the fact remains that no one quite knew it was happening—except, of course, for Becca.

Because her father and I were both parish pastors at the time, Becca was cared for during worship by surrogate grandparents in each of our respective congregations. At Hebron Lutheran, the church my husband served, this role was filled by Betty Kanas, and at First Lutheran, the church I served, she was cared for by Clarence and Louise Bell. Throughout the time that I served First Lutheran, I observed Clarence and Louise care for Becca with unwavering joy and ease, similar, I suspect to the care they had shown their own children and grandchildren over the years. They cradled and fed her as a baby and, as she grew, adapted to her boisterous toddler phase seamlessly. By eighteen months old, Becca felt as at home in the parish naves of our two congregations as she did in our own house. She skipped up and down the aisles between services, ran her toy trains along the edges of the pews, greeted every member of the choir with energetic waves, and giggled with glee when she was granted the opportunity to "test out" a new key or stop on the organ.

Nevertheless, each week she was at First Lutheran, when the worship service began, Becca was steadfastly seated in between Mr. and

Mrs. Bell, often balanced just barely on the edge of the pew or teetering on her tiptoes to see what was going on at the altar. The Bells, together with Betty, taught Becca to hold a hymnal, sing even when she didn't know the words, and fold her chubby fingers in prayer. And, of course, they always brought her forward to receive a blessing during Communion.

We used a large loaf of fresh-baked bread for Communion in that parish. The bread not only looked and tasted delicious, but its aroma would often fill the nave before and during worship. As the presider, I tore liberal pieces from the fluffy interior of the loaf as I distributed it. In retrospect, it's not at all surprising that right around the time Becca's love of good bread emerged, she also realized that what was being shared among the adults was far superior to the goldfish crackers in the snack cup she carried.

I don't know for sure, but I suspect that upon this realization, Becca pretty quickly voiced her complaint to Louise about the injustice of not receiving her own piece of bread. She was, after all, at that same time also discovering the power of using her voice to make her wants known, as every toddler does. What I do know is that one day, after breaking off a piece of bread for Clarence and Louise in turn and laying my hands upon Becca in blessing, I walked past them to the next group at the altar rail and observed, out of the corner of my eye, Louise breaking her large piece of bread in half and offering one of the pieces to Becca.

Not a word was ever said about what I observed. Yet from that day forward, after saying words of blessing over my daughter's head, I broke a piece of bread from the loaf itself, as I did for every other communicant, placed it in her hands, looked her directly in her eyes, and said, "The body of Christ given *for you*." I don't know whether Louise thought of it the same way, but I believe that by sharing bread from the Communion table with Becca, she was sharing the gift of Christ's body already. What shifted when I began handing Becca the bread directly wasn't her experience in the communion of the saints—that much was already secure. By giving her the bread from the same source and with the same words as everyone else, however, I was signaling that truth to both her and the gathered community with clarity. This was affirmed by the lay assisting minister that day (and every Sunday following) who, without question, seeing me commune Becca with the bread, did the same for her with the cup by handing her a cup of grape juice with the words "The blood of Christ, shed for you."

Under the circumstances, my daughter's desire for inclusion in the eucharistic feast isn't that remarkable. She behaved in the same manner as countless children whom I have observed over the course of my ministry and participation in parish life. Free of the inhibitions socialized into us as we grow, toddlers see something that they want, and they naturally reach for it. What really took my breath away wasn't my daughter's brazen demand for the eucharistic bread, but her caregiver's unhesitating decision to share it with her.

I suspect that if I had asked Louise at that time, or any time before or after, about her opinion regarding First Communion, she would have likely insisted that instruction be given to children at a sufficient age of reason so they can understand the sacrament properly. Although the specific age and notions of proper understanding have shifted across generations, I know that this is the general practice by which each of the Bells and their own children received their First Communion. It was also the practice of our parish and, despite theological statements affirming the availability of Communion for *all* the baptized, it is still today considered by many people to be "good order" in our denomination.

This is why I doubt that Louise was intending to commune my toddler when she first broke her bread and shared it with her—though I intentionally never asked. Nor did Louise ever ask me why I began "officially" communing Becca after that day. Rather, in that moment of eucharistic sharing, what is perhaps most significant is that Louise was acting to *include* my daughter. Seeing a child aching for something so simple for her to provide, she instinctively shared from her bounty. And whatever they may or may not have thought about young children receiving the Eucharist, Louise, Clarence, and even Betty continued to share this bounty for the entirety of our time in those parishes—bringing Becca bouncing joyfully up to the eucharistic table, teaching her to extend her hands at the rail to receive the bread, and assisting her with little cups of grape juice every Sunday. Indeed, even when the elements themselves are not shared, I see this same instinct among parents and grandparents who allow their children to place their little cups in a basket after they (the adults) have consumed the contents, pastors who lovingly clasp the outstretched hands of toddlers and little children at the Communion rail, and youth workers who offer packaged snacks or trinkets to children who come forward in worship. The message is clear: all are welcome.

Inclusive Ministry

While the details may differ across contexts, I don't think that Louise Bell's impulse to include my daughter was unique. Most adults want children to feel included. We want to share the good gifts of God's grace with the next generation. Moreover, study upon study conducted by church growth organizations indicates not only this desire but the *need* to include children and families in religious communities for the sake of the health and future of the church. Jesus praises "whoever gives even a cup of cold water to one of these little ones" (Matt. 10:42); in most churches, a person who would avoid this sort of small grace is rare indeed, especially outside of the worship space itself. In the fellowship and Christian education wings, churches abound with people like the Bells, who boost toddlers so that they can view buffet tables, help children to extra cookies at potlucks, carry Life Savers in their pocketbooks for restless preteens, assist with crafts or vacation Bible school singing, and share their bread when there is plenty to go around.

One might ask, then, what is the problem? Why do we need another book about children and the church? This book establishes that children were important to Jesus and the early church and makes the case that children should continue to be important to the church today. But at least at some level, we already *know* that children were important to Jesus and that they should remain important to the church. The implicit assumption of every graph that reflects how the average age of churchgoers has increased over the past two generations and every church ministry discussion oriented around how to attract families or children is that *children are important in the life of the church.*

There is little to no question about whether children should be included in the church or its ministries. I suspect that for most of you, committed perhaps to children's ministry or faithful parenting or a combination of both, the answer is a resounding *yes*—of course we care about including children in the church! This book is, in fact, written out of gratitude for you.

The question as I see it isn't about *if* children should be included in the church, but rather *how* to fully include children—and not only in the church as a collection of buildings or ministries, but more fundamentally in the church as the collective gathering of the body of Christ. In the various congregations that my family and I have had the privilege of being part of, whether for a short time or a long time, I've never encountered a lack of passion or energy for the inclusion of children and their families. This, with no small thanks to faithful families and youth workers, we are blessed with in abundance.

However, over the course of our children's lifetimes, bringing them to worship both as their pastor and, in other contexts, as a solo parent in the pews while their father led worship, I have often encountered disagreements or outright paralysis over what including children means, not just for the children and their families themselves, but for the entire congregation. I have observed a disconnect between the sort of *intuitive inclusion* I describe above, which I think describes the good intentions of most congregations to welcome children, and the more expansive *full inclusion* of children not just in a corner of the building dedicated to children's ministry or at Wednesday evening youth events, but in the corporate life of the whole community.

This book is about bridging that gap. It is about seeing the outstretched hands of the children in our churches and responding to them with compassion. It is about seeing in their hands not only a need to be met but the ability and desire to share and to serve. Full inclusion means the shift from caregivers surreptitiously sharing their bread to Communion ministers confidently proclaiming, "This is the body of Christ / This is the blood of Christ, given *for you*." And then, perhaps even more dramatically, it is a shift to allowing those same children to place the bread in *our* hands and to experience the incarnate Christ when they say, in return, "This is the body of Christ given *for you*."

Our daughter, Becca, was nine years old the first time she stood in front of the altar holding the common cup, offering the blood of Christ, in the form of grape juice to the worshiping body. Because she is a petite child, as adults came forward to dip their bread in the cup she offered, it was necessary for some to stoop a bit to partake, no matter how high up her small arm extended the cup forward. As smaller children came forward, I noticed the smile on their faces as they were able to look Becca straight in the eyes as they easily reached the cup she extended downward, hearing the promise of Christ's presence declared for them. Yet whoever received Christ's blood from Becca that day, whether young or old, short or tall, received the same promise and the same presence.

This is what it means to be, together, the body of Christ. Full inclusion of children in worship is not just or even primarily about the children. From a theological perspective, worship is participation in the communion of saints; it is about gathering as Christ's body *together*. It is about reaching out to one another, whichever direction we need to extend the welcoming hand. Full inclusion means accepting that we are all members of one another, working together with, rather than in opposition to, one another for the sake of the realm of God. Most of all, embodying the body of Christ means acknowledging that when a segment of that body is missing or is somehow relegated to the side, as children can be, then the whole body suffers. As Paul writes, "If one member [of the body suffers], all suffer together with it; if one member is honored, all rejoice together with it" (1 Cor. 12:26).

Inclusive Scripture Reading

Paying attention to each member of the body is the goal of inclusive Scripture reading. Such readings are embodied in beautifully diverse ways by interpreters who embrace their God-created uniqueness through feminist, womanist, masculine, disability-oriented, Latin American, African American, and queer readings of the Bible, just to name a few. As a mother and biblical scholar focused on the inclusion of children, I wrote this book in an effort to do the same through a child-centered interpretation of Scripture.

Moreover, just as inclusion of children in worship is about the whole body of Christ, so too does centering children in Scripture reading lift up the whole body—adult and child. Through attention to children in our reading, I believe we can reorient our approach to one another at an intergenerational level—children and adults—as stewards of the same heavenly realm, members of one body in Christ. The goal, then, is not to privilege children over and against adults. Rather, the novelty in a child-centered reading of the Bible is simply that it doesn't immediately privilege adults. The use of the term *childist* sometimes applied to such readings isn't intended to imply bias of any kind either in favor of children or adults, nor is seeking out the children in Scripture meant to be a gimmick to attract young people's attention or offer adults a fresh way to read the text. Child-centered, or childist, interpretation seeks to learn equally from both the children and the adults in the biblical texts by paying attention to the presence and experience of all the characters in the story, even the children who are too frequently forgotten or assumed to be adults.

Typical readings of Jesus' teachings on children provide a prime example. Each Gospel author tells the story of Jesus blessing real, actual children. However, most adult Bible studies on this story focus on how adults can *be like* these children in order to enter into God's realm, rather than lifting up the experiences and contributions of actual children in God's realm. At the same time, Sunday schools are filled with posters and story Bibles that make it clear Jesus blessed and welcomed actual children. With the exception of the occasional intergenerational event, contemporary churches are generally structured to keep adults and children apart, not only in worship but also in Scripture study.

In contrast, out of necessity, adults and children shared far more space in the ancient world. Taking place in this context, Jesus' ministry assumed the presence of *both* adults and children more often than not. By reclaiming the roles that children played in Jesus' ministry, the child-centered interpretations that follow seek to shine a light on how much adults and children each have to learn from one another. Child-centered reading seeks to learn both from and with *all* of the little ones who believe in Jesus.

Strategies for Reading

Part of the nature of this focus on the needs of one another is that there is no single pioneer of this child-centered approach to reading biblical texts. Rather, child-centered readers have, over time, discovered that we share similar strategies.[1] These strategies aren't intended to be hard and fast rules but, rather, guides to help shine a new light on children both in and beyond the biblical narratives.

The first of these strategies I've already mentioned. It involves shifting the focus from adults to children. This shift is not about privileging children but about opening ourselves up to seeing children in the text. Instead of assuming that every text is written solely for adults or that every character *is* an adult unless otherwise specified, childist readers ask the questions "How would a child perceive or read this text?" and "Where might the children be *in* this text?"

Next, a childist reading pays attention to the place and role of children in the biblical world. As we read the Gospels, this means asking about the roles and responsibilities of the children whom Jesus encountered in their own world. Since Jesus and most of his followers were Jewish, this means paying attention to the roles and responsibilities of children in first-century Jewish culture. Since the Gospels take place during a time of empire in the area now known as Israel/ Palestine, attention to context also means asking about the place of children within this larger cultural context, including North Africa, Roman Italy, and other locations across the Mediterranean basin.

The final two steps of childist readings of biblical texts are aimed at leveling the playing field between adult and child readers. The biblical texts were written mostly, if not entirely, by adult men who, often without even knowing it, inherited the adult-centered, patriarchal worldview of their cultures. They have also been widely interpreted over time by adult scholars whose work, to varying degrees, represents similar adult-centered biases in the contemporary world. Such readings run the danger of repeating the mistake of placing stumbling blocks in front of the very little ones whom we seek to welcome into Christ's presence (Matt. 18:6).

To correct for this adult-centered bias, child-centered readings don't just lift up the child characters directly named in the Bible; they also look for children in the shadows of the biblical narratives—children who may have been present and unnamed in houses, crowds, synagogues, or streets. Paying attention to the places children commonly inhabited in the first-century world, a child-centered reading of the Gospels can fill in gaps left in the actual text in order to understand where children may have been, even if they aren't specifically mentioned. The most frequent example of this involves remembering the children present in the crowds, as in John's feeding narrative (John 6:10; cf. Matt. 14:21); however, this can also occur by inquiring deeper into the background of unnamed children, such as the child whom Jesus places in his disciples' midst (Matt. 18:2).

Finally, as we notice the presence of children, either directly stated or emerging from the gaps of the Gospel stories, childist readers attempt to respect these children as human beings in all of their fullness. This means not stopping at recognizing the ways in which adults act toward or speak for children, but paying attention to how children themselves act and speak in the stories. In this way, child-centered readings are committed to seeing the interactions between adults and children in all of their complexities. Children are more obviously dependent upon their caregivers and their environments than adults, but paying attention to children helps us to see the interdependencies between all human beings and God's creation. It is to such relationality that Jesus commends those of us who seek to follow him when he instructs his disciples to be like little children (Matt. 18:3).

At the same time, such an instruction was never meant to be an either/or. Jesus does not intend to exclude either adults or children from following him or entering the realm of God. The ways in which adults and children work together in this ministry can be reclaimed by recognizing child disciples where adult-centered readings do not commonly see them—for example, in the person of John, son of Zebedee (Mark 1:19–20), or Mary, sister of Martha (Luke 10:38–42). In this way, by living into God's covenant with God's people—both adults and children—Jesus continues to extend God's blessing throughout his ministry and commands his disciples to continue in the same way.

Unfortunately, somewhere along the line, as the early followers of Jesus separated from Jesus' earthly ministry and from Judaism, they also lost this intentional focus on supporting one another across all differences—especially age. By recentering our attention on the real children impacted by Jesus' teachings on children, a childist rereading of these familiar texts paves the way for even more genuinely inclusive interpretations that can open us up to different understandings of what it means to relate to one another as members of the same body.

As we apply these principles of reading to additional stories from Jesus' life and ministry, it is my hope that our imagination for different kinds of relationships made possible by Jesus' directive both to welcome and become like little children will blossom. This child-centered interpretation is grounded on the belief that both adults and children can benefit spiritually from paying closer attention to the ways in which children participate in and contribute to the building up of God's realm as they are portrayed in the biblical texts. When we look again at Jesus' teachings on children through this lens, it becomes clear that Jesus is no more silencing adults than he is silencing children. When Jesus commands his disciples to welcome children in his name, he does so with a view of a community that is big enough not only to hold but to welcome and affirm all of God's people—including both children and adults.

In this way, child-centered readings of the Gospels have the potential to benefit the whole body of Christ as we imagine anew what it means to uplift and support one another—adults and children—in all our diversity. For too long, children have been commanded to keep silent not only in church but anytime they are among adults. This expectation for children to fade into the shadows has led to precisely that. The task before us as adult readers is to let the little children come to *us*, as we discover together what it means to live into the realm of God, with all the gifts God has given us to share.

Coming Together as the Body of Christ

I call my daughter's unintentional Communion a blessing of the best sort because in that moment of unpremeditated acceptance God cut through all the barriers and welcomed her as God's child into the full fellowship of the body of Christ. In that act, the *whole* body benefited. I believe that in that moment and through a shared love for both Christ and a child, our small congregation was gifted with the "greater gifts" about which Paul writes (1 Cor. 12:31). These gifts can take many different forms, but at their heart they are centered in love for God and one another. Such love is embodied in full inclusion and acceptance of every member of Christ's body, across all our intersecting identities, including age.

Defining Welcome and Inclusion

Different congregations and denominations live into this fellowship of Christ's body in different ways. The point of this book is not to persuade you that any one sacramental theology, form of gathering, or way of being is better than another. This is not a book about sacramental practice or a how-to book on Christian education or First Communion, nor is it a book about how to parent young children from the pews or the best approaches to including and reaching youth in worship. It is my hope that this book may spark your imagination around these and many other topics related to the roles of youth and family in church. Most importantly, though, this is a book about community. Specifically, it is a book that celebrates what is possible when adults and children come together in community as one body in Christ.

It is necessary to affirm that this inclusion extends across race and ethnicity, gender and sexuality, wealth and poverty, ability and disability, geographic location, and chronological age. Recently, many mainline churches have gravitated toward stating, "All are welcome," often intending to counteract the assumption of LGBTQ exclusion in Christian churches. However, the expansiveness of this welcome and what it means to live fully into such welcome is often taken for granted and so not embodied in the life of the church either for LGBTQ worshipers or others. As a White, cisgender, heterosexual, middle-class Euro-American woman, I find that mainline congregations (which are themselves predominantly White and middle-class) generally welcome me with ease. But sometimes I arrive at many of these same congregations as all of those things *and* as a slightly frazzled mother with my small children in tow and am greeted with a different response. While I typically experience the same verbal welcome, when I come to worship with young children, acceptance into the community and, in particular, into the worship space may be on much shakier ground. In the early years of my parenting, more than one fellow Christian walked back that welcome because I allowed my toddlers to stand on the pews, I nursed my infants in worship, and I sat toward the front so my children could see.

I highlight my personal experience as an example of the larger challenge—the full inclusion of children into the body of Christ, however your community embodies this grace. Whether yours is a tradition that baptizes or dedicates, communes toddlers or teenagers, invites children to sing with the praise band or color quietly in the pew—whatever human identities and experiences your congregation actively affirms or is working to understand, I am convinced that God is calling each of us to take seriously the children in our midst, not just as the future of the church (though they are surely that) but also as gifted and essential members in the present body of Christ.

From my studies of the Bible, I am convinced that children and adults have labored side by side in the body of Christ since the very first followers of Jesus. The idea that children were important to Jesus isn't itself a radical claim; it's the centerpiece of such beloved children's songs as "Jesus Loves Me" and "Jesus Loves the Little Children." But when we talk about Jesus' love for the little children, we have a tendency to sentimentalize his love, like we would a child's love for a stuffed animal or a cute kitten. In contrast, to recognize children as integral members of the body of Christ alongside adults speaks to a deeper and more participatory kind of love. Children were not simply loved by Jesus in a one-directional way. Jesus recognized children as equally capable of returning that love. In love, Jesus recognized the gifts that children brought—and continue to bring—to the community of believers.

But Jesus wasn't the first or only one in his community to affirm these gifts. Although the world of Jesus' day was different from our own in many ways, the communities in that time and place were teeming with children and with families and neighbors who valued those children. On a daily basis, parents, grandparents, and community members entrusted their children not only with their livelihoods but with the respect and continuation of their traditions. Deuteronomy 11:19 records God's command to the Israelites to teach God's promises "to your children, talking about them when you are at home and when you are away, when you lie down and when you rise."

Children were central to God's promise to the Jews; as Jews themselves, both Jesus and his disciples knew and honored this. Jesus' love for children was not unique to him, but a part of his Jewish identity and heritage. Sometimes we can miss this generational value in the first-century world, though, because of cultural differences between the United States of America in the twenty-first century and Galilee and Judea in the first, and part of the purpose of the studies that follow is to bridge this gap. Honoring and loving children in Jesus' context looked very different from what most twenty-first-century adults think about when we imagine honoring and loving children today, but it remained a central value of the Jewish faith.

Defining Children and Childhood

While Jesus and his community affirmed and welcomed children, the truth is that there is no single way to do this. Growing up on a farm is different from growing up in a city, and cultural assumptions around childhood are as varied as the number of cultures we encounter. Talking seriously about children and childhood is thus heavily contextual and requires a series of assumptions from the start. I am writing from my experience as a White American mother and cannot authentically do otherwise, which means that the cultural assumptions I make about childhood come from this context. Even more specifically, I grew up and have raised my children in a middle-class, dual-income household in small towns and suburbs of the United States of America. These contexts influence my view of childhood.

Within White American suburbia, childhood is often sentimentalized and idealized, with a view that children ought to remain innocent and avoid work as long as possible. Parents often try to "protect" children from the "real world" or curate their activities in an effort to tailor their future success. Such desires, while mostly well-intentioned, have been embodied in intensive styles of child-rearing that have been described as "helicopter parenting" or "snowplow parenting"—attempts to protect children and to remove obstacles from their way, respectively. In its extreme, this kind of parenting made the headlines in 2019 with a college admissions scandal involving numerous high-profile White celebrities in the United States.

Even in a more moderated approach, such parenting styles mark economic privilege due to the amount of time, energy, and money they consume. My culture is thus characterized by a fierce intentionality in marking off childhood as a protected space completely separate from adulthood.

Foreshadowing this cultural understanding of childhood, French historian Philippe Ariès famously argued that there was no concept of childhood in ancient societies before the Renaissance. Other historians of family and childhood have since pointed out the cultural limits of Ariès's study, as well as the error in his assumption that childhood must be carefully distinguished from adulthood in order to exist. The result has been more nuanced discussions of *childhoods* in the plural, rather than a monolithic, timeless standard for childhood. While I write from my experiences of childhood, therefore, I do so with an ear toward and awareness of the multiplicity of experiences of childhood both past and present.

In many such experiences of childhood, the distinction between adult and child is nowhere near as neat or complete as White American suburbia or Philippe Ariès might have us think. In most instances in the ancient world, childhood and adulthood were distinguished not by age or physical maturity but by one's place or role in society. Most typically this involved marriage and procreation, though for boys some level of adulthood might have been realized when they established themselves in a field of work even before marrying. In contrast, in the United States today, childhood is usually legally defined with reference to age rather than social status. However, at what age one is classified as an adult continues to vary, with tiered ages at which a person is legally recognized as an adult in the United States. This standard is actually set at the state level, with most states setting the age of majority at eighteen but permitting individuals certain mature privileges, such as driving, as early as fifteen or sixteen and, despite allowing a person to serve or even be drafted into the military at eighteen, not permitting the consumption of alcohol until the age of twenty-one. Meanwhile, medical studies on brain development and functioning suggest that most people don't reach full maturity—and so don't have the ability to fully assess risks and consequences—until the age of twenty-five.

Thus, while early childhood is easily identified through biological immaturity, by the time a person reaches early adolescence, the stage where individuals increasingly interact in community, childhood and adulthood are identified mostly by cultural rather than biological markers. And these cultural definitions can vary widely. Young adults in U.S. suburbia today grapple with when and how to define this transition, celebrating mundane milestones from doing the laundry to ordering pizza to paying the electric bill as "adulting." More officially, adulthood is often celebrated when a young person graduates from college, rents their first apartment, or begins a full-time career.

At the same time, one of the great threats to Black American youth today is the adultification of Black youth by White-dominated culture, leading to the oversexualization of Black girls in the media and the criminalization of Black boys by police. The assumption in White American culture that some (White) children need special protection while other (Black) children are dangerous is not only empirically wrong but insidiously dangerous. This has led to the persistence of courts to try children, especially Black or other racially minoritized children, as adults in the criminal justice system. The legal default at which individuals are assumed to be adults, and thus capable of being held fully accountable for their actions in the criminal justice system, is eighteen. However, judges are given the discretion to shift that standard down, depending upon the state, with various states setting limits between ages ten and fifteen and others setting no lower limit at all, allowing children as young as seven or eight years old to be tried as adults. In highlighting the gifts that children bring to the church, it is particularly important for White Americans like myself to recognize both the youth and the giftedness of Black and Brown children *as children*. Combating this cultural evil of inappropriately labeling developing children as adults is one of the important tasks of reading again familiar Bible stories with an eye for children in mind.

In short, human development is a process that occurs over time. This makes it difficult to define the transition between childhood and adulthood with a concrete number, as much as we may try, and accounts for some of the ambiguities we will encounter when attempting to locate individuals who may have been socially defined as children in the Gospel stories. In this task chronological age can be helpful, but paying attention to social roles and positions is much more telling—especially in stories that rarely reveal their characters' ages. Although the key ages and social markers differed, cultural distinctions were also what most readily marked the transition between childhood and adulthood in the first-century Mediterranean world. For both boys and girls, puberty and adolescence were a large factor in this transition, especially when tied with marriage and procreation. But these were not the only social markers of adulthood. For Jewish boys, successful Torah study and inclusion in ritual obligations at twelve years old was a significant step toward adulthood at the religious level, although their adulthood was not yet fully realized on a social level. For Roman boys, the transition to manhood was heavily attached to completion of required service in the military, usually at around eighteen years old, or to their ascendancy as head of their household when their father died. Rarely, young women whose parents died without any male heirs would fill a similar role.

However, the most definitive markers of the transition from childhood to adulthood across gender and cultural differences had to do with one's role in the household. For a boy, this often had to do with greater economic contributions related to completing his education, performing military service, or mastering a trade. Such milestones equipped a young man with the ability to responsibly marry and provide for a wife and children. For a girl, adulthood was closely tied to taking on the roles of wife and mother associated with marriage and childbirth. Because of these factors, girls typically married once they reached child-bearing age, somewhere between twelve and eighteen years old, while boys waited until they were able to provide for a family, marrying on average about five to seven years later than girls. While there continued to be some ambiguity as young people passed these milestones, by the time they were parents in their own right, they were unquestionably considered adults.

Part of the task of reading for inclusion of children is to recognize that cultural difference is not the same as social position. In Jesus' world, children are depicted as moving about more freely in the Gospel stories and at a younger age than many readers today would expect, but that does not mean they ought to be counted as adults anymore than a ten-year-old latchkey child would be considered an adult today. Culture and context dictate what is safe or necessary for children and these vary between communities, times, and places, but they don't change the embodied reality of childhood. Children staying home by themselves or moving freely through the marketplace are still children and rely upon various support networks, including neighbors, extended family, and—today—technology to help care for them when their parents need to be away.

Another difference is that while there are now laws in place regulating when and how much children can work in the United States, it was not uncommon for a child in Jesus' world to hold what we would consider to be a full-time job. This was both because families needed all the help they could get in order to produce enough food and income to survive and because jobs in this preindustrialized economy would have been much easier and safer for children to perform. The stage of life designated as "childhood" also represented a shorter time in Jesus' world than it does today, for similar reasons. But at its core, childhood both then and now has to do with an increased dependence upon others, while maturity is often defined by greater levels of independence and individual responsibility, although different cultures privilege this experience of independence differently, with many Indigenous American, African, and Asian cultures in particular prizing community and interdependence over and against the individualism often touted as achieved adulthood in White America.

Noticing Children in Christ's Body

Observing such differences from a distance, some commentators on the New Testament have speculated that the first-century world valued children less than we do in the twenty-first century. It is true that the first-century world sentimentalized children less. However, I am convinced that a close reading of Scripture reveals that these communities valued children as much, if not more, than many Christian communities today. The key is in recognizing that in the first century children were not simply valued as precious innocents to protect, but rather as gifted participants in their communities of faith. Children, together with adults, were fully entrusted with God's promise.

Although it would be idealistic to say that children in the first century were fully included all of the time in their communities of faith, I have found that the biblical texts have much to offer us in terms of what a fuller inclusion of children within our own communities of faith might look like. We need only approach them with hearts willing to receive. In what follows, I invite you to journey with me into these texts, some familiar and some less so, and to encounter them with a new appreciation for the gifts that the children in these Gospel stories bring, not only within the communities where their stories take place but also for Christian communities today. I invite you to recognize and embrace the legacy of these children who helped to build the foundations of the body of Christ.

To set this perspective, each chapter begins with a reflection on lived experiences of children in the twenty-first century. This is followed by a summary of a related Gospel story, attention to the role(s) of children in the text, and reflections on how reading with attention to children might draw adult readers of each story both to live into our own "childlike faith" and to come alongside the children in our communities in the process. The goal is that with a fuller appreciation for the active roles of both adults and children in the mission and ministry of Jesus, we—as adults and children seeking to further that mission and ministry today—might seek to embody more fully the body of Christ, recognizing the gifts that we each bring as essential members, one of another.

Through these stories, we will explore the ways children ministered in the first century and how they can do so today as preachers, evangelists, learners, stewards, and cocreators of both family relationships and the ever-approaching realm of God. In the process, I invite you to wonder with me at the diversity and promise held in such a reading of the first-century church and to consider the ways in which twenty-first-century adults and children work together as members of the same body.

Chapter One

The Gift of Participation

The Little Children and Jesus

"Whoever welcomes one such child in my name welcomes me."

—Matthew 18:5

Joshua loved church. I mean, he *really* loved church. He was baptized at Crown of Glory as an infant, and his parents brought him faithfully to worship there every Sunday. Like many suburban mainline congregations, Crown of Glory had a dwindling cradle roll and a strategic plan that highlighted the need to reach out to more families with children. So of course they loved Joshua and his family and celebrated both his birth and his baptism with enthusiasm.

As a part of their commitment to ministering to families, the congregation provided a staffed nursery during worship. But from the very first, Joshua preferred to sleep peacefully in his mother's arms, lulled to sleep by the songs and prayers in the worship space instead. By the time he learned to walk, stopping at the nursery wasn't even an option in Joshua's mind—worship was where the real fun was to be had! His mom says that even at age two, he already loved singing and learning about Jesus.

Because Joshua loved singing and wanted to see everything that was going on around him, his family sat in the front left of the worship space every Sunday. This pew positioned them perfectly so that Joshua could see the altar, pulpit, organ, and choir all without straining.

From that perch, Joshua would dance a little bit in his space when the choir sang a particularly uplifting song. During the quieter songs, he would sometimes flip through little Bible books or push his toy cars across the rug, but he was always listening. During the liturgy, one of Joshua's parents would often hold him at the hip so that he could see what the pastor was doing. Sometimes he would squeal a bit with excitement at the spectacle of it all. Other times, he would stare intently, taking everything in.

If, as can happen with little children from time to time, Joshua became too restless in the middle of the service, or if his excited squeal turned into a prolonged conversation or scream, one of his parents would usher him down the aisle and into the entryway to figure out what the matter was. It would be a lie to say that Joshua's presence in worship was quiet or free of distraction, but his parents did their reasonable best to balance Joshua's interest in worship with the needs of everyone else in the worship space. Even if he didn't get it perfect all of the time, already at two years old Joshua was learning when it was appropriate to sit or to stand, to be quiet or to speak out.

As he learned these rhythms, Joshua's favorite part of the Sunday service soon became the children's sermon. Although he wasn't old enough to fully understand all of what was being said during this gathering, he faithfully toddled forward to sit on the front step of the chancel every week. He grinned his megawatt smile at the pastor and the rest of the congregation, simply enjoying being a part of it all. When the message was over, he returned to his parents with the same smile on his face.

After the service, Joshua delighted in giving the pastor a high five, and he often had a question about something that had been said or done during worship. Other times, he just enjoyed watching nursery-rhyme videos on his mother's phone while the grown-ups would chat after the service. What seemed to be most important for Joshua was simply being a part of it all.

Then one Sunday his mother came to worship nearly in tears. She showed me a letter she had received that was anonymously signed "The Congregation." The letter was two pages long, but it amounted to a demand that Joshua utilize the nursery during worship or, barring that, at least sit in the back of the worship space. It insisted that the congregation loved Joshua but that worship just wasn't the right place for him at his age.

The letter detailed the ways in which Joshua was a "disruption" for others during the service. His quiet (and occasionally excited) vocalizations in worship were named, as well as the "distraction" of having to watch Joshua being ushered out of the worship space from the front of the room to avoid such noises. (This, it was noted, would be avoided if his family sat in the back pews, closer to the door.) The letter also stated that it was difficult for some of the older members to focus on the choir when they looked at Joshua dancing in his seat and that, in general, adults would be able to appreciate the worship service better if children, like Joshua, were not present.

Soon after, Joshua and his parents decided it was best to look for a different worshiping community. They found this visiting a neighboring congregation, Epiphany, where they were greeted by an enthusiastic explanation at the start of worship that "at Epiphany, *all* are welcome, and when we say all, *all means all!*" with the entire congregation chorusing the last part.

During a sermon one Sunday at this new church, Joshua found himself wandering in the aisle. This was something children in this congregation did from time to time, in no small part because when they tired of their explorations they were almost universally welcomed or greeted with a smile or a high five at whatever pew they found themselves near—whether their family was in it or not. However, on this Sunday, Joshua wandered a bit past the pews and found himself near the stage with the pastor during the middle of the sermon.

Without missing a beat, the pastor kept preaching and took Joshua's hand in a friendly gesture, gently guiding a slightly lost Joshua back to his parents, all the while continuing to preach. Nobody present even batted an eye; Joshua was not the first, nor will he be the last boisterous child to grace their worship space. In contrast to the community that welcomed him in words alone at his baptism, this community welcomed Joshua (and his family) into their midst without qualification.

Joshua's family learned the difficult way that the congregation at Crown of Glory loved the idea of children more than they loved real children—or at least more than they loved the practice of incorporating real children and families into their midst. Reality is often more complicated than ideals—and in the case of children, noisier too. But this conflict between the concept and practice of loving children isn't new. Jesus' followers themselves faced similar struggles.

Jesus Loves the Little Children?

In some ways, the divide between caring for children as a concept and as a practice was fundamental to the early Jesus movement. Jesus preached the ideal of caring for children, but some of Jesus' other teachings had the potential to put real children at risk. Jesus taught that complete devotion to God must take priority over every other commitment, including commitments to a person's family or children (Matt. 10:37; Luke 14:26). He also called his twelve disciples to leave everything, including their families, to follow him (Matt. 19:27; Mark 10:28; Luke 18:28), depriving their children not only of their parental care but also of the labor and income they would ordinarily have provided.

Within a couple of generations of Jesus' lifetime the conflict had increased in the church around balancing the ideals and practices of caring for children with a commitment to Christ. Some people within the church felt that Jesus' teachings, combined with an expectation that he would soon return, had made traditional families obsolete and so avoided marriage and childbearing. Supporters of this view found support in Jesus' pronouncement "Woe to those who are pregnant and to those who are nursing infants" in the last days (Matt. 24:19). A noncanonical early Christian story called The Acts of Paul and Thecla also favors this view, depicting Thecla as refusing marriage in order to be an apostle for Christ with Paul.

Other early Christians felt that such antifamily interpretations of Jesus' teachings were extreme. Proponents of this view argued that Jesus never intended for all his disciples, or even most of them, to abandon their families to follow him. As time passed and the church developed, these more moderate views supporting and maintaining family life ultimately held the most traction and were included in our New Testament. They can be seen in letters such as 1 Timothy, Colossians, and Ephesians. These letters include instructions for household management and relationships between parents and children, showing an early interest in families even if the ways that we conceive of and structure our family relationships have changed in the intervening years.

In Jesus' lifetime, however, the truth was probably somewhere between these two extremes. Children were valued in Jesus' world, and Jesus affirms this value throughout the Gospels. However, just as affirming and working for the embodied value of human life and dignity put Jesus' own life and dignity at risk in the short term, so too supporting and working for the embodied value of those on the margins—including children—could have the effect of putting some children at risk in the short term. This is the balance that Jesus' disciples seem to struggle with in the most famous stories about Jesus welcoming and prioritizing children. We will take a closer look at each in turn.

Jesus Places a Child in His Disciples' Midst: Matthew 18:1–11; Mark 9:33–37; Luke 9:46–48

In Mark and Luke, the scene for Jesus' first teaching on children is set by an argument between Jesus' disciples while they are traveling.[1] Having been on the road for a while already, the disciples have gotten to talking. In fact, their talking seems to have morphed into a competition of sorts as they quarrel over who is the greatest among them. Jesus notices the argument and takes it as an opportunity to teach his disciples about true greatness.

To make his point, Jesus gathers his disciples and places a little child among them. The famous translation in the King James Version describes Jesus as setting a little child "in the midst of them" (Matt. 18:2; Mark 9:36). Although the text doesn't say, the seemingly quick response to Jesus' call suggests that this child was somewhat nearby. Since children outnumbered adults two to one in the ancient world, it makes sense that Jesus would not need to go in search of a child. It's even possible that the child was traveling on the same road, either among or as one of Jesus' disciples.

Whoever the child is, he or she seems to come willingly when Jesus calls. And the disciples don't seem surprised by the presence of a child in their midst. Children, both on the road and in moments of teaching, were a part of the everyday experience of first-century Galilee, so the disciples don't object to this child's presence; they don't even pay the child particular notice. Instead, the Twelve, aware of their own special status among the larger group of Jesus' followers, are more self-absorbed in determining their pecking order, assuming that Jesus will name one of them greatest in his realm. In the context of the hierarchies they understand within the larger world, if they themselves are not greatest, it is likely they suspect someone with even greater privilege or connections with Jesus to be named—perhaps one of the patriarchs of the Hebrew Bible. Whoever they expected Jesus to name as "greatest in the kingdom of heaven," it almost certainly wasn't the child whom Jesus placed in their midst.

Yet Jesus instructs his disciples to be like this small child. And then he goes on to command them, at length, to care for such children. First, Jesus makes clear that welcoming a child such as this is the same as welcoming Jesus himself. This teaching is shared in all three Gospels. Matthew's account goes even further, with Jesus extending his teaching by adding severe warnings against creating stumbling blocks for or despising "these little ones" (Matt. 18:6, 10). The message is clear: children are important to God.

So it shouldn't come as much of a surprise when Jesus continues his travels from Galilee into Judea that there are children there too. Children are just one of several groups of people that the Gospels describe approaching Jesus in Judea. Crowds come for healing (Matt. 19:1), religious leaders come to test him (Mark 10:2), and still others bring little children that Jesus might touch them (Mark 10:13).

Jesus Welcomes the Little Children: *Matthew 19:13–15; Mark 10:13–16; Luke 18:15–17*

If the contemporary Sunday school had a theme passage, this would be it. Churches across the world depict this scene on the fronts of children's storybook Bibles and in murals and hangings adorning the walls in Christian education wings. Strangely, though, the adults bringing the children to Jesus are typically left out of these illustrations. Instead, children are portrayed encircling Jesus, sometimes in first-century clothes, other times in modern dress, often with various shades of hair and hues of skin. It's the embodiment of the children's song "Jesus Loves the Little Children."[2]

These illustrations seek to convey Jesus' love for children. However, in a rush to make Jesus' love unique and countercultural, they miss that the ordinary adults—the ones scrubbed from the scene in many illustrations—loved children too. In fact, the ordinary adults in this Bible story treasured the children in their midst so much that they took the extra effort to bring them out to meet Jesus when they heard he was beyond the Jordan. As faithful Jews, they likely took these actions out of a conviction that children are a blessing and an essential part of God's covenant. While many of these children may have been able to travel mostly on their own, adults in their lives have taken the time to guide them. Luke tells us that some of the children may even have been babes in arms, relying upon their mothers or nurses to carry them to Jesus. This too is a living out not only of basic parental obligations but of a covenant relationship between parents and children. As Jews, Jesus' disciples would have been readily aware of that.

What makes the children being brought to Jesus remarkable to some of Jesus' disciples isn't that they're young. Compared to others who are brought to Jesus in the Gospel accounts, what's most remarkable about these children is the fact that they don't appear to *need* anything. These children (and the adults who bring them) haven't come to ask Jesus a question or learn from his teachings. They don't appear to need healing. And Jesus hasn't summoned them, as he did with the child whom he called earlier into their midst. Instead, Matthew explains that these children are being brought to Jesus "in order that he might lay his hands on them and pray" (Matt. 19:13).

When Jesus' disciples turn these children away, it may not actually have anything to do with their age. In fact, Matthew isn't clear about which of Jesus' followers actually turn the children away. There may even have been children among the group of disciples turning these particular children away. If that is the case, it isn't only or even primarily the age of the children who are being brought to Jesus that presents the problem. In the eyes of the disciples, the biggest distraction may simply be that this group approaching Jesus doesn't seem to have big enough concerns. Understanding Jesus' mission to be one of teaching and healing, and perceiving these children not to need either, Jesus' disciples attempt to block them to protect Jesus from unnecessary distractions.

Jesus' core group of disciples was likely particularly attuned to the need to avoid distractions to Jesus' ministry, as this figured highly in his teaching. When Jesus sent his twelve disciples out to proclaim the gospel, Mark says that "he ordered them to take nothing for their journey except a staff" (Mark 6:8a). When he called his disciples to follow him, they often left their own homes and families in order to answer this call (Mark 1:16–20). In Luke's Gospel, Jesus is even quoted as saying, "Whoever comes to me and does not hate father and mother, wife and children, brothers and sisters, yes, and even life itself, cannot be my disciple" (Luke 14:26).

Reading this statement in light of the whole ministry of Jesus and his disciples, commentators have speculated that the point Jesus seems to be making is the need to prioritize God and God's realm above everyone and everything else. Sometimes this may have required leaving one's family; sometimes one's family might have come along on the path of discipleship. However, the hard truth is that Jesus' call to discipleship almost certainly demanded sacrifices on the part of his followers' families, including their children. In all three Gospels where Jesus names these stakes, his disciples reply, "Look, we have left everything and followed you" (Matt. 19:37; Mark 10:28; see also Luke 18:28). Coming from a Jewish culture that valued care for one's family above everything but worship of God, this affirmation illustrates just how high the stakes are for the disciples in following Jesus. They are committed to preventing any distractions from Jesus' primary mission.

At the same time, it is important not to misinterpret this prioritization of the realm of God with a necessary stigmatization of children. Following in the Jewish tradition, Jesus' teaching about leaving households was more about commitment in general than it was about the distractions that children, as one particular group in a larger household, might provide. And this teaching was focused for the Twelve as a select group for the specific time of Jesus' earthly ministry. More broadly, Jesus makes clear that having children among the community with whom he ministers is not only acceptable but desired. Jesus demonstrates that all those who trust in him, regardless of their particular needs, are welcome to receive his blessing. Jesus reproaches his disciples: "Let the little children come to me, and do not stop them; for it is to such as these that the kingdom [*basileia*]of God belongs" (Matt. 19:14). Here again, as in his teachings about the child in their midst, Jesus reorients attention away from what his disciples think is most important and toward a child, or in this case, many children. Such a radical shift eschews the values of kings and kingdoms in favor of a less hierarchical structure embodied by my colleague Ron Allen's translation of the Greek word *basileia* as "realm." Jesus doesn't merely tolerate the children who are being brought to him, but he affirms the value their caregivers have placed in them and raises the stakes by declaring that the realm of God around which his whole ministry is based actually *belongs* to such as these.

Children in the Story

The Child in the Midst

In Matthew's Gospel, the disciples' question about greatness comes on the heels of another discussion between Jesus and his disciples—this one about whether it is proper to pay the temple tax. The temple tax, although offered in the Jerusalem temple, ultimately benefited the Roman government. This is why, when Jesus instructs his disciples to pay this tax, he reasons that doing so avoids offending "the kings of the earth" (Matt. 17:25). Since economic power was and is a huge factor in greatness, at least in worldly terms, the disciples' question is likely related to this discussion.

New Testament scholar Eunyung Lim has demonstrated that Jesus' answer, too, seems to build upon his earlier teaching. She explains, "When hearing about the sons of the earthly kings and their exemption from tax obligations, Matthew's immediate audience may have remembered those sons of the Herodian dynasty who [were sent to away to be educated in Rome and] spent a much more protected and privileged youth under Rome's cloak than most of the children in the province of Judea."[3] In his explanation of the taxes, then, Jesus draws a comparison between the children of the kings of the earth and the children of God. Just as the children of earthly kings are free and protected, so the children of God are free and protected and, by implication, owe tribute to no one. Jesus doesn't instruct the disciples to pay the temple tax as a matter of obligation, but rather, out of their freedom, to keep the peace. This is a fine line, because it protects the disciples from potentially dangerous consequences if they refuse to pay the tax while at the same time suggesting that true greatness lies outside of these human powers.

The greatness that Jesus has in mind isn't contained in castles or treasuries, but rather in relationship. The word translated as "children" in Jesus' explanation of the taxes isn't directly related to age as with most of the Greek words translated as "children" in the New Testament. The word in this exchange more literally means "sons." Children, in this sense, refers to a lifelong relationship between children and parents. The disciples agree that the kings of the earth protect and care for their children. So too, by implication (indeed, all that much more), God the heavenly sovereign protects and cares for God's children.

In the disciples' experience, such protection led to status and privileges of not only the sons of emperors but also the family of Jewish elite, like Herod's household. Most if not all of Jesus' core followers came from work-a-day households that would have never known this kind of privilege. So it's only natural that when Jesus begins to reframe their image of who the real sovereign is and invites them to envision themselves as children of the "king," they begin to dream.

Such dreaming leads to the same self-oriented imaginings that the disciples come to more directly in the accounts by Mark and Luke. If greatness awaits them in the realm of God, Jesus' disciples want to know who will be the greatest. In response to their question then, however it is conceived, Jesus places one of their smallest traveling companions in their midst. If the disciples were imagining rubbing elbows with royalty and kings, Jesus calls their attention to someone who likely has even less status than them—in fact, possibly the very least status or privilege at all.

We've already seen the ways in which first-century children were treasured and cared for within their families, embodied by those who bring them to Jesus for blessing. However, from a power perspective, children still ranked at or near the bottom of household hierarchies. These hierarchies assigned power according to a variety of factors, including gender; age; wealth; citizenship; and whether one was free-born, freed, or enslaved. Because of this, it's impossible to create a precise ladder for social status. For example, a free Roman woman held more power than an enslaved noncitizen man, even though, all things being equal, men were higher up in the hierarchical order than women. However, all other factors being equal, the lower a child's age or birth order, the lower that child ranked within the household hierarchy.

On top of this, because the child whom Jesus places in his disciples' midst is on the road together with them, it's possible that he or she may not even have a household within which to determine a place in the hierarchy. The child may have left a household to follow Jesus. Many people followed Jesus, even from the start of his ministry in Galilee (see Matt. 4:25; 27:55). And even more people joined the crowds who listened to him in whatever city or village he found himself. Because of this, it's possible—even likely—that the child Jesus places in the center of his disciples comes from this larger discipleship group of Jesus' followers. Some even think that the child may have been the little boy from whom Jesus had just cast out an unclean spirit in the previous episode (Luke 9:37–43). Even more drastically, the child may not have a household to connect with—lost either through parental death or abandonment. By all expectations, the child whom Jesus calls to himself is the furthest from any worldly definition of greatness that the disciples could imagine. While the disciples are dreaming of elevating their status by their roles as followers of Jesus, Jesus tells them instead they must humble themselves even further (Matt. 18:4).

Despite contemporary applications, humility (in Greek, *tapeinos*) as Jesus understands it is about social status, not personal pride. To become humble or make oneself humble literally means to be made lower or to turn away from worldly prestige or status. At the most basic level, it is to make oneself vulnerable, to admit reliance upon other human beings.

Jesus emphasizes this vulnerability and dependence in the teachings that follow. To place oneself on the margins as a child requires that one receive welcome and hospitality rather than be the one who has the privilege and power to offer it. In the case of the adults who complained about Joshua disturbing their worship, it would mean restructuring their point of view to ask how they might help Joshua and other children to feel more connected to worship, rather than worrying first about themselves. To lower oneself as a child makes one vulnerable to stumbling blocks and reliant upon others to prevent or remove such obstacles.

The Children Jesus Blesses

Ironically, despite Jesus' warnings to the contrary, his disciples themselves continue to create stumbling blocks for actual children who seek Jesus. Even as Jesus instructs the disciples to be like children in his previous teaching, he never diminishes the personhood of the actual children whom he calls the disciples to model themselves after. Indeed, Jesus goes out of his way to instruct his disciples to care for and protect children.

When, not that long after, Jesus and his disciples encounter a gathering of children and the disciples attempt to prevent them from approaching Jesus, it seems as though this is yet another example of the disciples having missed the point. The disciples should have known better. By this point in his ministry, Jesus not only has instructed them to be like children but has healed several actual children whose parents have brought them to him for help. And his disciples did not attempt to prevent them. The disciples themselves received children who needed healing (Matt. 10:1; 17:14–20).

The issue at stake when the disciples rebuke those bringing children to Jesus in this instance then may not have anything to do with the fact that they are children. As we've already seen, by this point in Jesus' ministry, large crowds are following him, including children. Meanwhile many others are coming to Jesus for healing or to test his teachings, and some of the accounts of these healings include children. When in the middle of all of this a group of people attempts to bring seemingly healthy children forward for Jesus to pray over, the disciples may simply see themselves as conducting crowd management. After all, both Mark and Luke tell the story of a man who is paralyzed initially being unable to get to Jesus because of the crowds surrounding him (Mark 2:1–4; Luke 5:18–19). It is possible that the disciples are simply trying to triage those most in need of seeing Jesus, and healthy children don't make the list.

There is a temptation among Christians to read the story of Jesus welcoming the little children and want to paint the disciples as the villains, assuming that Jesus (and so Christianity) put an end to such exclusions. Practical theologian Bonnie Miller-McLemore critiques both the historicity and ethical dimensions of this tendency, surveying contemporary commentary on Jesus and the little children alongside historical and biblical evidence, and concluding that while it cannot be conclusively proven "that Jesus did not 'love all the little children of the world' . . . social, historical analysis of Jesus' ministry does suggest that he had his mind on less child-friendly agendas."[4] The more difficult truth is more complicated than a story of villains and heroes. On the one hand, the ideal of love and care for all people is routinely affirmed across most world religions and certainly is affirmed in Judaism as Jesus practiced it. On the other hand, those on the margins or those who don't fit in with the attitudes or behaviors of the majority have always been and still are routinely excluded. They don't make the list. Even as we attempt to deconstruct such lists of who is deserving of Jesus' love and care, Christian churches today continue to replicate the disciples' exclusions, oftentimes without realizing it, when they say "All are welcome" but have certain unspoken caveats to that welcome.

To break free from this trend toward hindering and to truly welcome and include children in our midst, it is helpful to pay attention not just to the disciples' words of exclusion but to what motivated them to attempt to prevent the children from coming to Jesus in the first place. In so doing, we may see similarities with our own contexts and may learn from their example to avoid falling into the same or similar traps in our own ministries.

Why then are people bringing the children forward to begin with? In Jesus' world, due to the higher threat of illness or injury to children, parents often sought prayers or blessings as a means of protecting their infants and young children. It was particularly common among Gentile parents to place ritual necklaces around their children's necks or statuettes in their rooms to ward off sickness and danger. These ancient talismans served many of the same functions that the concept of guardian angels do for some Christians today. Some Jewish parents participated in these rituals too.

In addition, as we have seen, Jewish culture and history is rich with traditions of blessing children, traditions in which Jesus and his disciples were steeped and in which the gospels suggest they continued to participate. Psalm 127 declares, "Children are a heritage from the Lord, offspring a reward from him" (Ps. 127:3), a theme routinely repeated throughout the psalter. The Torah contains multiple accounts of children who receive blessings for various reasons, including the young grandchildren of Jacob, Ephraim, and Manasseh, who are the first to receive their grandfather's blessings, ahead of his adult children (Gen. 48:8–22). And the prophetic mantle was given to Jeremiah in his youth (Jer. 1:1–10). Jewish parents throughout history have routinely blessed their children within their homes, and later traditions confirm that it was the practice within early rabbinic Judaism for children to be brought to the elders and scribes for blessings.[5] Moreover, such blessings typically involved a laying on of hands, just as Mark and Matthew describe.

By all appearances, then, the children who are being brought to Jesus in this story are ordinary children. They have no pressing need, but those who are bringing them value them enough to want to give them the opportunity to receive a blessing from Jesus as a known teacher and miracle worker. Such a blessing may have been understood in a protective sense, similar to the talismans many families invoked to protect their children from danger or even sanctify their future. Their very presence testifies to the intersections between the value and vulnerability of children in the ancient world.

But more than this, the little children who are brought to Jesus are a model of the kind of interdependency toward which Jesus has already commanded his disciples, through the example of a child. On the one hand, the Gospel authors make clear that the children are accompanied by adults. The children are the object, rather than the subject, of the opening scene; they are *being brought* to Jesus. Luke emphasizes this point by including the detail that people were bringing "even infants"—babies who couldn't yet walk—to Jesus (Luke

18:15). This implies a need or dependency upon others, likely parents or other caregiving adults in their lives, to both know about and get them this close to Jesus. Here we can see more parallels with the man who was paralyzed, who required the help of his friends in order to get close to Jesus.

But the children do not remain passive throughout. Instead, when Jesus rebukes his disciples, he calls for them to let the children come to him. This shifts the action from the adults who were bringing the children to the children who are now summoned to come to Jesus themselves. While the children may have required the help of others in their lives to get them to this point, Jesus recognizes that they are also able to come to him on their own from here. Some illustrations of this story even imagine that it is some of the older children who carry the babies in their midst these last steps into Jesus' presence.

In this way, we see that while children may need the help of others more than a typical adult, they are not solely passive and dependent. I imagine them responding to Jesus' call in much the same way Joshua responded to the call to come to the front of the church for a children's message. All of the children, especially the youngest in their midst, may not have fully understood who Jesus was or all of what he was saying. However, they knew from those who had brought him this far that he was someone whom they could listen to and trust. And they were willing to take part in the action necessary to come to him. Indeed, some of the children may even have brought their accompanying adults with them the final steps into Jesus' arms. In this way, the dependence of each member of Christ's body on one another—young and old—is put on clear display.

The Little Ones of God

When it comes to biblical words for "children," the word *mikron*, translated here as "little ones," probably has the widest range of meaning. In describing both the little one whom Jesus places in his disciples' midst and the children to whom Jesus promises God's realm, the Gospels use age-specific words that suggest a little child between the ages of three and seven, or in the case of Luke, even younger. However, in the extended teachings on children in Matthew, Jesus shifts his language, commending his disciples to care for "these little ones [*mikron*] who believe in me" (Matt. 18:6).

"Little ones" is pretty much a direct translation of an adjective that describes someone or something that is small in stature. Although it isn't directly related to age, it was a common way of referring to children in the first-century world—just as people today may fondly refer to a young child as "little one." Yet some people may call their children or grandchildren their "little ones" well into adulthood as a term of endearment. Unlike the more specific word for "child," this term, while it typically refers to young children, can refer to any number of people who are considered "little" for a variety of reasons.

In this case, Jesus' teaching about "little ones" occurs immediately on the heels of his teaching about an actual little child. Just before shifting language, Jesus says, "Whoever welcomes one such child in my name welcomes me" (Matt. 18:5). In light of this, interpreting Jesus' next teaching about preventing stumbling blocks as an expansion of what it means to welcome little children makes sense. This is especially true since these same themes return when Jesus reprimands his disciples for preventing the little children from being brought to him and welcomes them to himself in Matthew 19:13–15. Because of these connections, it seems likely that Jesus is talking specifically about actual children when he tells his disciples to avoid placing a stumbling block in the way of one of these little ones.

But this doesn't mean that Jesus is talking *only* about children. If Jesus' disciples follow his advice and become like little children in terms of their social and political standing, then they too could be considered "little ones." In the previous passage, Jesus has in fact instructed his disciples to do just that—to become humble, or "small," like a little child. In relation to Jesus' adult disciples, then, "little" can relate to their humble position in the world, since they have relinquished all power and status. The disciples, if they follow Jesus' commands, will be marginalized and even reviled; although "great" in the realm of God, they will be considered "little ones" in a worldly sense.

This meaning, which assumes faithfulness on the part of the disciples, might explain why Jesus shifts from talking about children in a general sense to talking about faithful children at this point in his teaching. In contrast to instructing his disciples to welcome *all* children, Jesus cautions them specifically against putting "a stumbling block before one of these little ones *who believe in me*" (Matt. 18:6, emphasis added). Jesus doesn't seem to be concerned with children as a general group anymore, but rather with those specific little ones who want to be connected to him. This certainly seems to include the disciples.

Elsewhere in Matthew's Gospel, Jesus also seems to use the term "little" as an affectionate term for his disciples. He says, "Whoever gives even a cup of cold water to one of these little ones *in the name of a disciple*—truly I tell you, none of these will lose their reward" (Matt. 10:42). "In the name of a disciple" (NRSV) is the most literal translation, but historically this phrase has often been translated as "who is my disciple" (e.g., NIV), largely based on the larger context in which Jesus is instructing his disciples about their ministry.

It may never be entirely clear whether Jesus is referring to his adult disciples when he cautions against placing a stumbling block in front of "these little ones" or affirms those who offer a cup of cold water to them. This is especially true if we allow ourselves to recast our assumed vision of Jesus' discipleship group, as we've begun to do, to have included actual children. However, what *is* clear in each of these texts is that if Jesus does intend to include the adults among his disciples in his teachings about "these little ones," it is because those adults have abandoned their status and privilege in favor of humbling themselves like little children as Jesus has taught.

Since adults are included in the "little ones" whom Jesus seeks to protect on account of their becoming like children, it makes sense to assume that actual children would also fit into this group. In fact, since the term "little ones" more frequently refers to young children than it does to marginalized or humbled adults, it feels almost illogical to assume that Jesus' teachings here would exclude children.

Instead, Jesus' attention to *both* actual children and adults whom he calls to become like children makes it difficult, if not impossible, to separate the meanings. And such separation doesn't seem necessary to the story. When Jesus speaks of "these little ones who believe in me," he seems to mean both actual young children, such as the one he placed in his disciples' midst, and adult disciples who humble themselves, abandoning quests for status or power in order to become like children.

Once again, we see the artificial barriers that present-day churches attempt to create between adults and children begin to break down. The "little ones" who believe in Jesus are united because of shared relationship, both with one another and with Jesus. Children are naturally dependent and the adults included in this group have already set aside their claims to power and control, increasing their own dependence. Taken as a group, together these "little ones who believe" are thus free to rely upon one another.

Embodying Welcome in the Body of Christ

In each of these famous stories, Jesus lifts up the giftedness of children. At the same time, these stories aren't simply about children. They are about the participation of children *alongside* adults in the interdependent body of Christ. Jesus connects the entire realm of God with little children through a final teaching that applies to both children and adults: "Truly I tell you, whoever does not receive the kingdom of God as a little child will never enter it" (Mark 10:15; Luke 18:17). This teaching, although it has occasionally been applied in a literal sense (often in relationship with infant baptism or dedication), is typically understood by adult readers metaphorically to mean that adults must become like children to enter God's realm. This interpretation is at the center of Jesus' instruction to his disciples in Matthew's Gospel, which elaborates: "Truly I tell you, unless you change and become like children, you will never enter the kingdom of heaven" (Matt. 18:3).

Applying different stereotypes of childhood in the twentieth and twenty-first centuries, commentators have speculated that to be "like children" might involve qualities such as humility, trust, purity, innocence, dependence, or even marginalization. Some of these stereotypes fit first-century views of children better than others; in any century, however, stereotypes and generalizations *about* children are very different than the lives *of* children.

But Jesus' teachings in Matthew's Gospel don't stop with the metaphorical. Jesus goes on to teach about welcoming actual little ones in his name. The word he uses here literally refers to someone who is small in stature and is typically applied to actual children or those who are of a low or marginalized status like children. In either case, Jesus makes clear that to receive one such as this is to receive Jesus himself. The same thing happens with Jesus' warning about placing a stumbling block in the way of one of these little ones.

In their hearts, most followers of Jesus, including contemporary churchgoers, want to stop stumbling blocks from preventing those who believe in Jesus from receiving his blessings. The trouble is that too often, like the disciples, we imagine *ourselves* as those who need this protection. Yet Jesus doesn't offer these words *for* his disciples alone. Jesus actually addresses the command to prevent little ones from stumbling *to* his disciples, with the idea of them removing barriers for other little ones in mind.

Followers of Jesus are not entitled to obstacle-free worship or access to God. Rather, Jesus calls us to humble ourselves and to remove barriers for *one another*. Churches today that make space for both children and adults in their worship model this sort of barrier crossing. In such community worship, some adults may have to make accommodations for children like Joshua, but at the same time, it is recognized that at many points in communal worship, children are accommodating the preferences of adults. When everyone takes into consideration the needs and preferences of one another, the worship experience is enriched. For example, when my family attended Epiphany Church together with Joshua and his parents, there were some songs that had my young children out of their seats, dancing along with the band. These typically weren't my favorite, but I experienced the Spirit by watching the children interact; there were other more traditional hymns that were meaningful to me, during which my children colored quietly as the congregation sang. Even then, however, there were times when my daughter colored a small picture, such as a flower, which she delivered to other congregants seated near us. Once, an elderly couple sitting across from us received one of my daughter's flowers during the sharing of the peace. Later this couple told me that they experienced the Spirit through her that day. That was a good day and one on which I was glad I insisted on sitting in the midst of the assembly with my children—in complete transparency, however, over the multiple years and congregations in which I worshiped with young toddlers, there were also days when I had to work hard at maintaining a quiet but pleasant balance with my toddlers in the front pew, and still other days when I recognized my children's restlessness and discerned that it was in the best interest of both them and the congregation for us to worship from the provided cry room.

Recognizing our relationship together, adults and children, as the body of Christ demands that we remove the stumbling block for our neighbor *before* we complain about the stumbling blocks in our own paths and that together we welcome those who, due to their perceived lack of power or influence, often have the hardest time getting their voices heard. This is what it means to live into the body of Christ simply because it is what it takes to keep all the body's various members together. However, at the same time, such actions can reap glorious rewards.

When our son, William, was in kindergarten and just beginning piano lessons, his preteen sisters were already relatively accomplished young musicians. The children's minister of my spouse's congregation reached out to see if one of our daughters would be interested in providing the musical accompaniment for "Silent Night" in the annual Christmas program. Both girls declined—the eldest because she was too busy with schoolwork to learn a complicated arrangement and didn't want to perform an "easy" piece, and our middle child because she prefers not to perform in front of crowds. Upon hearing us discuss the invitation, however, their brother proudly proclaimed that he would be happy to do it. We hesitated at first, not certain whether William's beginning piano skills were quite what the children's minister had in mind, but due to his eagerness and insistence we eventually asked the children's minister what she thought. With a wisdom greater than ours in that moment, she said yes. The result was an adorable and beautifully played duet by my husband and son to accompany the other children's singing. Not only did William nail his performance, but in the context, it turned out that his simple arrangement was more suited to the program than anything either of his sisters may have done. Our preconceived notions of what was appropriate for church could have deprived William and the congregation of that performance, but thankfully, William's willingness to share his gifts prevailed.

With the benefit of hindsight, when I reflect on the reactions to Joshua's participation at the congregation where he was baptized, I believe that the adults who confronted Joshua's parents were afraid. Like me anticipating William's piano performance, perhaps they simply didn't know what to expect. Perhaps they were concerned about creating a disturbance. And although they may not have articulated it so starkly, perhaps they were afraid that if there was a place for Joshua in their congregation, there may no longer be a place for them. They were afraid that by fully welcoming Joshua into worship they would be creating stumbling blocks for their own worship. Because of this, adult members asked Joshua's family to sit farther back in the church. They asked that Joshua remain in the nursery to prevent the occasional toddler noises that made it difficult for adults to hear the sermon. Effectively, they were asking the "little ones" to remove potential stumbling blocks from adult disciples rather than the other way around. What they missed was both the need for Joshua to have his own stumbling blocks removed, and the potential for children like Joshua, William, and so many others, to help bring others to Christ just as surely as any other adult worshiper in the collective body.

I don't believe that the members at Crown of Glory realized that by asking Joshua's family to make these accommodations they were inadvertently placing the very barriers that they were attempting to remove for themselves in Joshua's way instead. In fact, they may have reasoned that by spending his time in the nursery Joshua would have the opportunity to build community more effectively with children his own age. The trouble—and the gift, if treated properly—is that there aren't multiple bodies of Christ according to age or developmental status. There is only "one body and one Spirit" (Eph. 4:4). And although sometimes separate worship or activities according to age, gender, or interest groups may help to build relationships, most of the time Christian community is best built as a unity among diversities.

In the nursery, even if they are surrounded by wonderful toys and books, children miss out on the community and experience of worship altogether. And adults miss out on the equally important experience of worshiping together with children. Some congregations attempt to find a balance between these extremes, bringing the nursery children into worship to share in the eucharistic meal with their families, or creating a children's worship time outside of the main worship service that is directed toward the youngest members of the body. Depending upon the context and the child, these can be good and worthy adaptations; however, as we consider Jesus' desire to remove barriers, the important point in any context is that children and their families *choose* what adaptation works for them.

When that choice of whether to gather in community with a peer group or in an intergenerational body is removed from a child for the sake of adults who want to transform the one body in their own image, the body as a whole is injured. The father of an adult man with autism at Epiphany once told me about his experience being asked to leave a previous congregation as his son grew older and his need to wander around the worship space during services persisted. At Epiphany, both father and son regularly served as greeters and acolytes and were fully welcomed into the church body. Their previous congregation lost out on the gifts that they brought because they were not able to see beyond the immediate noise and disruption.

Similarly, because they were afraid of their own injury, the members of Crown of Glory inadvertently injured the worship body that they were a part of. Because they saw Joshua as a stumbling block, they accidentally added stumbling blocks for him. The members of "The Congregation" who wrote that letter may not have realized it, but the farther back small children sit from the "action," the more difficult it is for them to see and the easier it is for them to lose focus. The less interaction they have with the pastor, worship leaders, and other members of the congregation, the less likely they are to develop meaningful relationships with them. The members of Crown of Glory may have been afraid of losing connection, but inadvertently they caused just that.

This is because adult fears about children disturbing the balance of worship assume that the experience of worship is a zero-sum game—a scenario in which either adults or children can fully participate in worship, but the two cannot do so together. On the other side of this scenario, this is also what we imagine when we erase all the adults from our illustrations of Jesus blessing the children and then only feature those portraits in the children's Sunday school area. But that isn't how God works. When Jesus welcomes little children to him he doesn't do so at the expense of his adult followers. If we read the text again more carefully, we see that when Jesus calls the little children toward him, he doesn't send his adult disciples away. Jesus demonstrates that there is room for both adults *and* children in God's realm. When Jesus says the realm of God belongs to children, he isn't suggesting a tyranny of children at the expense of adults. Instead, Jesus is embodying a radical reprioritization of the needs of those who are most vulnerable. And when Jesus invites his disciples to humble themselves and be like children, he reminds the disciples that by recognizing their own vulnerability, they can find space in God's realm too—not over (or under) anyone else, but in relationship together as one body, both adults and children.

This is the worldview that the congregation at Epiphany embodied when they welcomed both Joshua's family and the family of the young man with autism into their midst. The mission statement and grounding principle of this congregation is that all are welcome. By welcoming a little child (or, for that matter, many children) into their midst, they embodied Jesus' teachings. However, extending welcome to people who may be excluded elsewhere does not mean existing members are no longer included. Fully welcoming children need not privilege little children to the exclusion of adults. (At the heart, this is what I think the members of Crown of Glory feared Joshua's family might be demanding.) Instead, the affirmation "All are welcome" recognizes the truth that the group of little ones who believe in Jesus includes all who are willing to humble themselves to make space for another.

By trusting this promise, Joshua's family found their home in a community of inclusivity. "All are welcome" includes both children and adults. Worship at Epiphany didn't prioritize children. If it had, that might not have been the right fit for Joshua's family, since Joshua thrived around the preaching, singing, and music making of faithful adults. But remarkably, worship at Epiphany didn't prioritize adults either. Epiphany made equal space for bell choirs played by adults *and* children, with the appropriate instruments for each. The preaching was primarily directed toward adults, but there was space for children to engage and interact—or to simply relax and feel affirmed and loved. The freedom of movement and participation at Epiphany allowed for both adults and children to be enriched by and to enrich the worship with their own strengths and in their own particularities.

At Epiphany, the body of Christ is embodied in all of its rich diversity as *one* body. Members of one another, people across age and ability, race and ethnicity, gender and sexuality, recognize their need for one another in this embodiment of God's realm. Through such relationships, power and status are no longer the primary concern, and so pride and privilege begin to drop away. This is how Jesus envisions the realm of God. Often this vision is translated in Scripture as the "kingdom of God." But the Greek term *basileia* can be translated to describe a kingdom as a power hierarchy, like the Roman Empire, or as "realm" to describe a range or domain of space. In this inclusive vision of worship and ministry, the term "realm" fits better with Jesus' promise to make little children its keepers and topples the power-driven hierarchies usually associated with monarchs and kings. By giving God's realm to little children and calling adults who want to follow him to become like children, Jesus inaugurates a radically different kind of kingdom. In God's realm, people don't compete with one another; rather, we *care* for one another—all because Jesus directs our attention to the little children in our midst.

Jesus' ministry with children isn't about division or exclusion; Jesus embodies the inclusive nature of God's promises to God's people when he calls the children to come to him. Jesus welcomes both adults and children, modeling full inclusion across the generations. Jesus teaches that in the realm of God, greatness is counted not based upon how powerful and privileged a person may be independently, but rather on how one relates *interdependently* to another. It is belief in this full participation and contribution of each person that was at the core of first-century Jewish families like the one Jesus was raised in and was likely instilled into Jesus himself from his birth.

For Further Reading

Garroway, Kristine Henriksen, and John W. Martens, eds. *Children and Methods: Listening to and Learning from Children in the Biblical World.* Leiden: Brill, 2020.

Gundry, Judith M. "Children in the Gospel of Mark, with Special Attention to Jesus' Blessing of the Children (Mark 10:13–16) and the Purpose of Mark." In *The Child in the Bible*, edited by Marcia J. Bunge, Terence E. Fretheim, and Beverly Roberts Gaventa. Grand Rapids: Eerdmans, 2008.

Lim, Eunyung. *Entering God's Kingdom (Not) Like a Little Child: Images of the Child in Matthew, 1 Corinthians, and Thomas.* Berlin: De Gruyter, 2021.

Lindeman Allen, Amy. *For Theirs Is the Kingdom: Inclusion and Participation of Children in the Gospel according to Luke.* Lanham, MD: Lexington/Fortress, 2019.

Questions for Reflection

1. What are the stumbling blocks that keep you from fully participating in the body of Christ? What are the stumbling blocks you observe that keep others in your congregation from this same participation?
2. Can you think of a time when as an adult you have needed a child (or as a child an adult needed you)? What was this like? Was the child aware of the support he or she provided?
3. When Jesus tells his disciples to "be like a little child," what does this mean for you? How can you strive to live into this command?
4. What gifts do children bring to the body of Christ in your local congregation? What gifts do children bring to the body of Christ in your larger community? In the world? How can you facilitate the sharing of these gifts by children and youth?
5. Jesus says that the realm of God belongs to such as the little children who come to him. He makes a little child among his followers an example of greatness in God's realm. What would it look like to take this seriously in our churches today?

[illegible]

For Further Reading

[illegible]

Questions for Reflection

[illegible]

Chapter Two

The Gift of Proclamation

The Bethlehem Shepherds

> "They made known what had been told them about [the Christ] child; and all who heard it were amazed at what the shepherds told them."
>
> —Luke 2:17b–18

Kom! Kom! Kom!" Khwezi shouted. "Kom! Amy! Kom!"

I couldn't understand his words; but I recognized his urgency. A large cloud of dust had gathered and was barreling toward us at an alarming speed. Later I would learn that this kind of dust storm was relatively common in the dry plains of southern Namibia, where Khwezi's family farmed, and that the best defense was to secure the farm and then wait out the storm indoors. In that moment, though, I simply knew that Khwezi was calling me.

Khwezi was my four-year-old host brother during my two-week homestay on his grandmother's goat farm. Not more than three feet tall, Khwezi had lively brown eyes that sparkled with a seemingly endless supply of energy and curiosity. He was a typical preschooler and a strong contrast to my nineteen-year-old self. At barely five feet three inches tall and 120 pounds, I still towered over Khwezi, but his grandmother continually worried that a strong wind might blow me away. My pale White skin left me vulnerable to the intense afternoon sun, but most of all, my look of complete bewilderment and confusion in the face of the impending storm left no questions about who, Khwezi or I, was in control of the situation.

It was the middle of the day, and the rest of the family had taken the donkey cart to work farther out on the farm, gathering, among other things, wood for our evening fire. This included Ouma, at seventy years old the matriarch of the farm; Nceba, Khwezi's twenty-year-old cousin, also a college student, who was spending her school holiday on the farm to assist with translating during my stay; and Joseph, a fifty-year-old man who lived in a neighboring compound on the communal land and whom Ouma hired to help with some of the heavier lifting. The task of gathering wood was deemed one of these heavier tasks, and so Ouma, Nceba, and Joseph had gone off to complete this, leaving Khwezi and me, the least experienced of the bunch, to tend to smaller chores closer to the house.

This had been a routine on other days and allowed Khwezi and me plenty of time to play together and teach one another games after we completed simple chores. Without Nceba present to translate for us, we couldn't speak with one another well. But with a few simple toys and my eagerness to learn everything about life on the farm, we found many ways to communicate and have fun. Khwezi, for his part, tolerated my failure to engage in conversation with him, which he earnestly insisted was all part of an elaborate ruse.

Up to that point in his life, Khwezi had met very few White people, and those he had met were all White Afrikaners, descendants of Dutch colonizers of South Africa, who spoke the colonial language, Afrikaans. Khwezi's family primarily spoke the Xhosa language, which was native to their region. But despite English having been adopted as the official language of Namibia at its independence, many people, particularly in the more rural parts of the country, still used Afrikaans for commerce and to communicate across regional languages and dialects. And so already at four years old Khwezi was bilingual, speaking both Xhosa and Afrikaans, as were his grandmother and Joseph. Nceba was trilingual, her university studies adding English to the two languages she had known since she was a child. In any case, in Khwezi's lifetime of experience, he had met few people who could not speak Afrikaans, and certainly none of them were White. So Khwezi reasoned that my failure to respond was simply an odd stubbornness that could be broken. With that goal, he kept speaking Afrikaans to me, sometimes sweetly, other times with passion, trying to trick me into a response. As my stay progressed, Ouma and Nceba had many laughs over Khwezi's growing frustrations; they both did their best to explain that I didn't speak Afrikaans, but he would not relent.

When the dust storm gathered, I had been staying with Khwezi's family for nearly a week. Up to that point, his frustration with our language barrier had served mostly as a bit of comic relief, not as a barrier keeping us from enjoying each other's company. While he didn't believe his family or me when we assured him that I could not speak Afrikaans, he readily accepted my desire to learn Xhosa and joined in teaching me Xhosa words for household items and simple requests. I suspect that for his four-year-old self this might even have felt like something of a novel game, teaching a teenager to communicate anew. Over the course of the week, he had even begun speaking to me less in Afrikaans, accepting that I would be unlikely to respond.

But in this moment, as the need to seek shelter from the storm persisted, Khwezi was once again shouting at me, this time urgently, in Afrikaans. What he might have thought of as a quirky game before had now lost its novelty in the face of real need, and his patience with me had run out. A storm was approaching, the rest of the family was a distance away, and he needed my help.

Although the goats would sometimes be led farther out on the communal land to pasture, at this time of day they were milling around the adjacent countryside, nibbling on bits of brush, and one of the tasks assigned to Khwezi and me was to look after them. Typically, looking after the goats didn't require much (if any) actual work, but with the dust storm imminent, it now meant herding the goats back to the safety of their pen.

As soon as he spotted the storm on the horizon, Khwezi halted our game, ran toward the flapping gate of the goat enclosure, and began shouting to me, "Kom! Kom! Kom!" At first, I stood rooted to my place, uncertain what to do or how I was supposed to help. Khwezi, I imagine, must have thought me hapless, and after a moment of frustrated exclamation, he quickly began the work that had to be done. Rushing to shepherd the closest goat with one hand, while holding the gate open with another, Khwezi continued shouting for my help.

"Kom! Amy! Kom!" Khwezi persisted. Finally, snapping out of my bewilderment, while still unable to comprehend most of the instructions that Khwezi was also shouting in short order, I got the idea that *this* word he kept repeating meant "Come!" In any case, the longer I observed my determined little host brother, the more obvious it was what he was trying to accomplish, and so I came running toward him, helping him to herd the remaining goats.

In the end, I failed miserably at rounding up any actual animals, but I was able to help simply by holding the flapping gate open while Khwezi cared for the herd, whistling and shouting and occasionally cajoling as the last of the goats finally followed him to safety.

When the last goat was within the fence, Khwezi noticed that I had no idea how to latch the gate, and so he secured it himself. Then for good measure he herded *me* into the house to wait the dust storm out. Once we were safely inside, Khwezi continued to speak in Afrikaans, I assume attempting to explain what had happened and what now needed to be done. I just stared at him blankly, and soon he threw up his arms in exasperation and found a game to occupy his time away from the willfully irritating housemate I'm sure I was proving to be.

Later, when the rest of the family returned but before I had the opportunity to get a word in edgewise, Khwezi rushed to greet them, eager to share his story. As he animatedly described our encounter with the storm, Nceba began to laugh heartily at his tale.

It was not unexpected that Khwezi was able to herd the goats appropriately in a dust storm; he had done so several times before. However, Khwezi's enthusiasm over sharing what he had seemingly discovered about me had his cousin gasping for breath. Once the laughter subsided, Nceba smiled at me and translated: "He says, 'See! I knew she speaks Afrikaans! When I called to her to help, she did what I said!'" So it was that Khwezi's opinion of me was cemented, with a conviction and enthusiasm characteristic of a child his age; my opinion of him was expanded, however, with a newfound respect for the expertise and resourcefulness with which he cared for his herd.

As I think back on this experience, Khwezi's expertise with that herd of goats stands in sharp contrast to the countless American children I have seen play the part of "shepherd" over the years in church Christmas pageants. It's not because Khwezi was, in general, any less playful or enthusiastic than any American child I've seen in a Christmas play. In our games together, Khwezi was frequently full of joy and energy. What strikes me is the way in which, in that moment of need, Khwezi channeled his energy so fully into the task at hand. The difference is not that Khwezi was an unusually capable preschooler. He certainly seemed to be a bright boy, and he was capable and confident in his tasks, but when I have observed other preschoolers entrusted with a challenging but reachable task, I have time and again seen many children rise to the responsibility as Khwezi did. I believe the difference is precisely in the trust with which my host family entrusted Khwezi—and me—with this work.

The quality of most Christmas pageants I have observed in the U.S. church context almost uniformly has less to do with the talent (or lack thereof) of the children and more to do with the trust and respect with which the pageant director treats the children. If a Sunday school teacher believes that a group of children is destined to goof off and distract each other, they almost certainly will. If that same teacher believes that those children are capable of memorizing lines, hitting marks, and singing solos, they almost certainly will do that instead. Khwezi's family believed that he could take care of the goats—and me—and he did not disappoint.

This sort of trust used to be much more common around the globe. However, with the rise of industrialization, many spaces have become less safe for children, and tasks that used to be possible for small children to complete have been complicated by computerization and machinery. Plenty of benefits have come with these changes, including the possibility in many places for children to attend school longer and with more regularity and, for some children, increased protections and opportunities for play. There is certainly an extreme risk to children when communities attempt to place adult responsibilities on young people who are not quite ready for them. However, an unfortunate result of this societal shift has been a gradual decline of adult expectations for children in cities and suburbs across the world. Children, however, have not grown less competent, as children in more rural and agricultural areas, like Khwezi, routinely show.

In these contexts, one of the gifts of playacting is the ability to entrust responsibilities to children in a relatively safe environment. Church and youth leaders would do well to understand the magnitude of tasks children not only are capable of but in which they have the potential to excel. Recognizing that children as young as four years old can and do shepherd real animals suggests that it is well within the ability of four- to ten-year-olds to act this part responsibly. Whatever their work—shepherding, acting, or anything else—the key is to recognize and affirm the giftedness with which children participate as a part of our faith communities.

The Star of the Christmas Pageant

Luke 2:1–20

We often think of the newborn Jesus as the "star" of the Christmas story; in fact, Matthew tells us God placed an actual star in the sky at his birth, shining down on him. Luke's telling of Jesus' birth lacks this detail, but Jesus remains the center of attention: *Jesus'* birth is heralded by an angel choir; shepherds seek the newborn *Jesus*; and after having seen *Jesus*, the same shepherds return to their flocks, glorifying and praising God.

Already at the nativity, it is Jesus who drives the action of the Gospel story. And this is the story children frequently act out in nativity plays. Yet to be the star, or title character, is not always the same as having the leading role. For example, characters like Godot in *Waiting for Godot* or the Wizard in *The Wizard of Oz* occasionally drive the plot more by their absence, or anticipated presence, than by anything they actually say or do. As a newborn baby, Jesus can't directly say or do much. So while Jesus is central to the story, he serves more as a silent star than an active lead. Knowledge of his existence drives the words and actions of others, even though Jesus says and does nothing himself.

It is actually the shepherds who play the leads in Luke's nativity story—shepherds who, like Khwezi, may not have been much older than the children who played them in your church's last Christmas pageant. These shepherds, albeit young and unnamed, are given speaking roles when even Mary and Joseph remain silent throughout Luke's account. Apart from the angels, the shepherds are the only characters with speaking roles. And unlike the angels, the shepherds show up in two of the three scenes of Luke's birth story: on the hillside and at the manger. Luke even follows the shepherds away from the manger as they return to the hillside again in what might be labeled an epilogue of sorts. In short, it is the speech and actions of the shepherds that move the story forward and help us to encounter and interpret the nativity event.

As if to intensify this point, the celestial light itself shines on the shepherds, rather than Jesus, in Luke's telling. There is no star guiding the shepherds to Jesus—instead, they are to seek him according to the angel's description given to them. The actual birth of Jesus is related in relatively plain speech—a child wrapped in traditional swaddling clothes, laid in a manger "because there was no place for them in the inn" (Luke 2:7). However, following this, Luke shifts the scene to the fields outside of Bethlehem, where no detail is spared to describe the angelic encounter the shepherds experience there. From verse 8 forward, the shepherds are the center of the action.

Luke tells us that they are keeping watch over their flock when the angel of the Lord stands before them. The glory of the Lord shines around them, and they are terrified. The angel speaks to them, proclaims that a savior is born to them, and declares as a sign for them that they "will find a child wrapped in bands of cloth and lying in a manger" (2:12). When the angels leave, the shepherds confer and say to one another, "Let us go now to Bethlehem and see this thing that has taken place, which the Lord has made known to us" (2:15). Then they travel "with haste" (2:16) and find Mary, Joseph, and the baby. After they had seen all this, "they made known what had been told them about this child" (2:17). Finally, they return, "glorifying and praising God for all they had heard and seen, as it had been told them" (2:20).

In short, from verses 8 to 20, the shepherds drive the action of Luke's nativity story. It is often remarked that the angel appearing to these ordinary workers to announce the good news of the Messiah's birth is a sign of Luke's attention to ordinary and marginalized people. This is true. But it is just as significant that it is these same ordinary, young shepherds who are the first human messengers of the Messiah's birth. And the shepherds announce this "good news of great joy" (2:10) not just to the residents of Bethlehem but to Mary and Joseph themselves.

The good news that the shepherds proclaim centers around the birth of a tiny baby, who the angels assure the shepherds is already the Savior and the Christ (2:11). Today Christmas is a feast of great celebration of the birth of a savior and everything that this savior came to mean in his life, death, and resurrection. But on that first Christmas, the shepherds didn't yet know the future that Jesus' ministry would hold; they didn't even celebrate the ascendancy of a young king or his anointing as future king. Proclaiming the infant Jesus, the shepherds and the angels celebrated God's presence in the world simply and sufficiently as a baby, gifted and chosen by God.

This striking chord of hope and celebration is highlighted by the shepherds' actions as they return from their visit with Mary, Joseph, and Jesus. Luke tells us that the shepherds return "glorifying and praising God" (2:20). Here, as throughout the angel's proclamations, the verbs used to describe the shepherds' actions are in the past tense, referring to actions taken by the angels and the shepherds in the moments surrounding Jesus' birth. The shepherds are not predicting or anticipating a future hope; rather, they are proclaiming and celebrating a present gift. They are reveling in the truth that on "*this day* in the city of David," a savior has been born (2:11).

Children in the Story

The Infant Jesus

The first and most obvious child in the nativity story is Jesus himself. Jesus entered into the world as a human baby—the same way we all do. The reason that he doesn't have much to say or do in Luke's nativity story is that, like any baby, Jesus is still highly dependent upon the adults around him. He relies upon Mary and Joseph to find a safe place for his birth, to provide him with clothing, to cradle him in their protective arms (or the security of the manger), to feed him, and to protect him from whatever other threats may arise.

Babies in any time and place are fragile and vulnerable. All babies require care and attention and are more susceptible than adults to disease and danger. However, in the first-century Mediterranean world, the infant and child mortality rates were especially high. Tim Parkin, a demographer of classical antiquity, explains, "To the ancient mind, the link between childhood and old age in demographic terms must have been that both were risky periods of life." Such that "in the ancient world, the first years of life might be associated not with safety but with danger: death was omnipresent as a threat."[1] Thus, even without the added threat of Herod's soldiers (Matt. 2:16), God entering the world in the person of an infant was a decided risk. Malnutrition and childhood illnesses, many of which were unknown or untreatable in this time, posed real threats. And babies, especially, were considered highly vulnerable, much more likely to die within the first week after birth due to prematurity or complications in the birthing process.[2]

Because of this, parents and communities celebrated births with cautious optimism, always aware that danger and disease were not far off. These risks were common even if a baby was born into the best of circumstances, which Jesus was not. Luke describes Jesus' birth as taking place away from home and the built-in support systems of family and friends, due to the imperial decree of a widespread census. Although there is no direct evidence of a census happening at this time and place, censuses within the Roman Empire were common as a way of taking account of imperial subjects for tax purposes. In this way, Luke describes Jesus' entry into the world as threatened from its very beginnings by the greed and power of empire.

Due to imperial forces beyond Mary and Joseph's control, Jesus is born away from home, with no room for them even in the guest room. The idea that Jesus is born in a stable, drawn from the detail that Mary laid him in an animal's feeding trough (Luke 2:7), has been overdramatized in most nativities. In first-century homes, animals were often kept on the first level, while the family slept upstairs, where there was often a guest room as well. This is the room (*kataluma*, often translated as "inn") where there was no space for the new family. Notably, Luke uses the same word to refer to the upper room that the owner makes ready for Jesus and his disciples near the end of the Gospel

(Luke 22:11). As a place for guests to stay, however, the lower level, which likely contained a feeding trough for the animals, was thus not as uncommon as contemporary nativities may lead us to believe. In the absence of modern heating and cooling systems, this room would have offered Mary and Joseph nearly as much shelter and comfort as the rest of the home. Still, the family's presence there, at the exterior of the household, represents a threat in a different sense.

Moreover, there may be another reason that Mary, Joseph, and Jesus were relegated to the exterior of the household. New Testament scholar Mitzi J. Smith follows in a growing trend of Lukan scholarship when she argues "that Luke's Gospel presents Jesus as the child of an enslaved woman."[3] In Luke's birth narrative, Mary identifies herself twice in conversation with the angel Gabriel. First, as a virgin (Luke 2:34) and again as a "servant of the Lord" (Luke 2:38). The Greek word that most English translations render as "servant," however, is *doule*, a word widely understood to describe "enslavement" in most other contexts within and outside the biblical text; indeed, even the word translated as Lord (*kurios*) most basically means "master." Thus, Smith quotes fellow New Testament scholar Clarice Martin, who "argues biblical interpreters and translators who render *doulos* as 'servant' obscure the fact that 'rendering service' was 'not a matter of choice' for the enslaved."[4]

And, since Luke gives no indication that Mary's enslaved status changes before Jesus' birth, Jesus is born into slavery also. Filling out this marginalized family, Smith proposes that "Joseph could have been a freedman or a free born master," but "either way, Joseph would have owned *and* been engaged to the young virginal *doule*, Mary" and one with little means, at that, since he is unable to afford more than the poor person's portion when he and Mary make their temple offering (Luke 2:24).[5] Locating Mary within the literal confines of enslavement can help solve the riddle of why there was no space in the guest room for a woman about to give birth. There was rarely, if ever, room in the guest room for an enslaved person. Indeed, a recent discovery of what has been dubbed "The Room of the Slaves" in Pompeii sheds light on living conditions of enslaved persons in the ancient world, noting that the cramped dark room was found "close to the place where . . . [a] vehicle was parked, and not far from the nearby stable."[6]

Making their literal and proverbial beds at the outer edges of the household, Mary and Joseph are thus depicted at the margins of the Bethlehem community. They are staying at the outer edges of the household that is sheltering them in a physical sense, and this marginality may be read to suggest that Mary and Joseph are also at the outer edges of the social support systems of the household in which they are staying. Had they remained in Nazareth, it might have been expected that Jesus' birth would have been attended by Mary's mother or other female relatives or midwives who were experienced and prepared to help with a birth. But Luke depicts only Mary and Joseph as present at Jesus' birth.

In their time and culture, it is unlikely that Joseph would have had the benefit of the proper knowledge or preparation to assist Mary. This lack of social support, in addition to the imperial threats we've already considered, makes Jesus' birth itself even more dangerous than it may otherwise have been. As a possibly enslaved baby born away from his hometown, during a census, at the edge of the household, without qualified assistance, Jesus is at risk. He is vulnerable.

This fragility doesn't take away from the care and celebration attached to Jesus' birth, though, even before the angelic choirs. The birth of any child in the first-century world was celebrated as a sign of a successful marriage, the purpose of which was primarily to produce offspring. Even more so, within Jesus' Jewish family, children were celebrated as signs of God's favor. As Mary's "firstborn son" (Luke 2:7), Jesus also received special priestly blessings, which Luke details when he describes Mary and Joseph bringing the baby Jesus to the temple shortly after his birth (2:22–38).

But even before these extended blessings—and, in fact, before Jesus' birth itself—Mary and Joseph knew that Jesus was not destined to be any ordinary child. As a child promised by God, Jesus was a special sign of divine favor, which Mary celebrates during her pregnancy in Luke's lyrical song known as the Magnificat (Luke 1:46–55). When they hold their newborn son, then, Mary and Joseph are aware both of his significance and value within their own family and the promise and hope he holds for the entire people of God.

Only a generation before Jesus' birth was announced, the birth of a different savior was proclaimed. This would-be savior was Caesar

Augustus, also dubbed a son of the gods. His birth was announced through official inscriptions and proclamations by (adult) soldiers and messengers across the empire, and the salvation that he offered was, through the imperial agenda, the chance to make the empire whole. Luke's inclusion of a promise of peace attached to Jesus' birth also parallels the propaganda that surrounded Caesar's birth. The peace that Caesar offered, however, was only for those who already held the privilege of citizenship and power. It fell to the rest of the empire to secure this peace, often through their own suffering.

The peace that Jesus' birth inaugurates, though, has a wider breadth. Early Greek manuscripts of Luke's Gospel record this proclamation in two different ways, and it's hard to know which was the original wording. The earliest Greek manuscripts use a word construction in Luke 2:14 that is most accurately translated as indicating that God's peace is directed toward "those on whom [God's] favor rests" (NIV) or "those whom [God] favors" (NRSV). However, other early manuscripts contain a word construction that is best translated as "peace, goodwill toward men," as in the NKJV, or "peace, goodwill among people" as in the NRSV alternate footnote. Without getting too far into the weeds of the grammar, these latter translations suggest a more inclusive scope—with God's peace extended to all people (the Greek word translated as "men" by NKJV most basically means "humans")—and not merely those whom God favors. However, when we take into consideration the magnitude of God's love, there probably isn't much of a difference. The distinction is more in degree, with an emphasis being placed on the experience of God's peace for those whom God considers "greatest"—the little ones, the ones, not uncoincidentally, least likely to have benefited from Caesar's peace (see Luke 17:2; 18:15–17).

Shepherds as Children

I've already alluded to the work of children as shepherds in agricultural communities, both today and in the past. The first-century Judean setting of Luke's nativity story is no exception, and so children working as shepherds were not unusual characters in the larger Jewish narratives with which Luke's audience was familiar. The most famous story of a child shepherd is probably of David, the youngest of Jesse's sons (1 Sam. 16:11; 17:15). When one looks a bit more closely, though, the role of children or youth tending sheep is assumed throughout the Hebrew Bible. The next most notable example, although often obscured by Christian English translations, is Rachel, who worked as a shepherdess caring for her father Laban's flocks (Gen. 29:6), although, as Hebrew Bible scholar Wilda Gafney notes, "the NRSV translation . . . reduces Rachel to merely 'keeping' sheep, without naming her as a shepherd, as do the JPS, GSJPS, and Everett Fox (Jewish) translations."[7]

Outside of the Bible, stories of young shepherds and shepherdesses grace both the folklore and the practical farming guides of the Mediterranean world and beyond. One of the better-known examples of such stories is Aesop's fable of the shepherd boy who "cried wolf." Its presence and staying power in the folklore of Greece dating back hundreds of years before Jesus demonstrates the pervasiveness of child shepherds both in the lived experience and the literature of the Hellenistic world. For generations, children the world over, like my Namibian host brother Khwezi, have been tending to small animals while the older and stronger members of their households complete the more strenuous jobs, and their work has been featured in stories and literature both directly and indirectly about them.

The reason for the prevalence of children as shepherds in agricultural economies is that sheep are relatively easy to herd. As a result, especially in small family farms in which the work of every able body is essential, the task of shepherding or the herding of other small livestock is within the capabilities of and therefore often delegated to the younger children. For small flocks and herds that typically stay close to the family home, this task can often be accomplished by one or two children on their own as young as four to six years of age. For larger flocks, a child between seven and ten years of age, or a group of shepherds, including both children and adults, is more common.

Luke didn't describe the Bethlehem shepherds like this because he didn't have to. Luke's audience, whether they lived in a city or more rural lands, would have been familiar with the role of a shepherd. Simply by locating the shepherds on the Bethlehem hillside, Luke paints a picture of a larger flock, or group of flocks, and so of a larger group of shepherds, including in their midst both adults and children, boys and girls, free and enslaved.

Nevertheless, the Bethlehem shepherds often remain an enigma to the present-day church. Small children play the part of shepherds in Christmas pageant adaptations of Luke's nativity story, often accessorized with cuddly plush sheep, and they occasionally show up in the illustrations of children's storybooks in the same light. However, apart from plays and books intended directly for children, most studies of or meditations upon the Bethlehem shepherds portray them as adults. Often the shepherds are even depicted as somewhat gruff or distasteful men to emphasize the contrast between their perceived social exclusion and the intuitive move toward inclusion that angels accomplish by delivering God's message to them. The narrative is often presented so as to imply that the world, including Judaism, excludes the shepherds but God includes them.

The idea that the shepherds may have been marginalized in first-century Judaism comes from an obscure reference in a sixth-century Jewish religious text called the Talmud. There is a section of this text that, although it isn't even the main point under discussion, includes shepherding as one among a list of occupations that had, by that point in the Mediterranean world, come under suspicion and mistrust. It is a stereotype akin to someone today saying that all bankers are greedy or all used-car salesmen lie. This single text hardly suggests that all shepherds were untrustworthy, and in fact plenty of alternate texts make quite the opposite point, including Jewish celebrations of King David and his humble origins as a shepherd boy written both before and after this portion of the Talmud.

Unfortunately, Christians, eager to understand how the Bethlehem shepherds fit into the larger nativity story, have often latched onto this idea that the shepherds were socially marginalized, even spurned or excluded as untrustworthy, so that we can then uplift these marginalized individuals as central to Luke's story of Jesus' birth and the full inclusion that this birth inaugurates. There is a much simpler explanation, however: the shepherds, as outsiders to Mary and Joseph's immediate family, are invited to become insiders to Jesus' birth, celebrating the importance of Jesus' birth not just for one individual family but for the whole of God's family on earth. In this view, the previous intuition toward inclusion implied by the typical narrative is expanded to a full and intentional inclusion of all of God's children, both within and beyond Judaism.

The expansiveness of this inclusivity is demonstrated by the fact that it is a group of shepherds who first visit after Jesus' birth. The Roman census forced Mary and Joseph to travel away from their home and close family and friends, the people one would have expected to attend their son's birth. Luke's description of John's birth, just a chapter earlier, explains that Elizabeth's "neighbors and relatives" visited and "rejoiced with her" (1:58) after her son was born. Although Jesus was born away from his parents' current home, he was born in the ancestral city of his human father, Joseph. As a result, a reader might still expect Joseph's extended family or friends, or even those who are staying in the adjoining rooms that offered the new family shelter for the night, to have been the first to visit after hearing about the child's birth. But those neighbors and relatives are surprisingly absent.

Mary and Joseph's separation from their family and other support systems is emphasized by Jesus' birth in a stable—at the exterior of the home where they were staying, among the animals. In contrast to Zechariah and Elizabeth, those who visit and rejoice with Mary and Joseph following Jesus' birth appear to be strangers. Whether or not they were on the margins of the larger Jewish community in Bethlehem, they were only marginally (if at all) related to Mary, Joseph, and the newborn Jesus. In a way, the shepherds foreshadow Jesus' later declaration that "my mother and my brothers are those who hear the word of God and do it" (Luke 8:21). In other words, family in God's realm is no longer limited by biological ties; Jesus' definition of family expands to include all of those who serve God. Responding to the angelic pronouncement, the shepherds definitely fit into this group.

There is therefore no need to imagine the shepherds as the metaphorical drudge of society in order to see the ways in which God is working, through Jesus' birth, to bring together the margins and the center of communities. By inviting the shepherds to celebrate at the moment when normally family and neighbors would greet a baby's birth, God is collapsing the boundaries between insider and outsider, beginning with the Holy Family. From the very start, Jesus' family is embodied by those whose words and actions align with the will and purpose of God, regardless of biological connection, economic status, or, of course, age.

Even as children, the shepherds are able to do the will of God by sharing their presence and their witness with Jesus and his family. This is remarkable in its own right. What's equally remarkable is the way in which they are received and welcomed by the Holy Family in this role. Children were valued in the first-century world, and it isn't even unusual that children would be gathered to greet a newborn infant following his birth. However, the role that these shepherds fill, strangers substituting for close family and children substituting for formal messengers, goes beyond these normal expectations, placing upon the youngest of these shepherds a weight of responsibility typically withheld until around twelve years old.

While young children were welcomed and valued in first-century Jewish religious life, their full inclusion in formal rituals, especially when it came to the weight of obligation, was a gradual process not all that dissimilar to that experienced by children in many Christian congregations today. Jewish boys, of course, were circumcised on the eighth day, just as Jesus was (Luke 2:21), but there were no further religious expectations placed on boys or girls during their infancy. As boys grew, although there is no strict record of age specifications for Torah learning in Jesus' time period, a slightly later midrash suggests that boys should begin to be taught the Scriptures around the age of three years old—as soon as they were able to begin praising God (nothing is said about Torah instruction for girls).[8] However, rabbinical teachings hold that neither boys nor girls were to be held to the full observance of the commandments in the Torah until they reached puberty.[9] Similarly, while the Roman Senate passed laws to protect and encourage families, even the children of the elite didn't show up to its meetings as speakers. In short, while children were included as members of both their families and religious communities and shared in the celebrations and work of each, then, as now, they were less frequently taken seriously for what they had to say nor always held accountable for it. This may be part of why Jesse doesn't think to invite young David, with his brothers, to meet Samuel in the first place, or why children in need of Jesus' help in the Gospel narratives are typically accompanied by parents who plead their case.

Shepherds are not the only young message bearers in the Scriptures. God calls Jeremiah to proclaim God's word as a prophet when Jeremiah is still a young boy. And yet Jeremiah's audience isn't initially as receptive as the shepherds' audience was. Jeremiah's primary objection to fulfilling his call is intimately related to his perception of his ability to proclaim God's word as a young person. He laments, "Ah, Lord God! Truly I do not know how to speak, for I am only a boy" (Jer. 1:6). Whether in Jeremiah's times or Jesus', young children weren't typically expected to be eloquent speakers.

Nevertheless, despite Jeremiah's objections, he becomes a powerful prophet for Israel, speaking the word of the Lord. Through the prophet Jeremiah, God demonstrates that youthfulness need not prevent a person from speaking God's word. And so, while still unexpected, by the time the shepherds are called, the precedent is set. All people, whether young or old, can proclaim the word of God. By tasking the shepherds with announcing their message of "good news of great joy for all the people," the angels, as God's messengers, once again demonstrate the power and effectiveness of child prophets called to proclaim the word of the Lord. And Mary, Joseph, and the crowds of Bethlehem receive their proclamation with trust and perhaps even enthusiasm.

This is indeed fitting for Jesus as a child savior, that the good news of his birth was not announced at first, or at least not primarily, to adults. The angels' message is given first to a group largely made up of children themselves—the shepherds tending to flocks of sheep in the hills outside of Bethlehem. Their presence and voices are brought from the margins of the Bethlehem hillside to the center of Jesus' story. And not only do these children respond, but they do so without hesitation, and all those who hear them are amazed. Mary herself treasures the shepherds' words and ponders them in her heart.

Mary as a Child

Whenever I ask students to name the children in Luke's nativity narrative, Mary always comes up. Unlike Jesus himself and the child shepherds, this description is a bit more complicated. Tradition has always treated Mary as a relatively young woman at the time of Jesus' birth. Recently, though, it has become popular to highlight that Mary herself was an unwed teen mother when Jesus was born. On the one hand, historically it is true that Mary was almost certainly in her teens when Jesus was born and the infancy narratives leave ambiguous the status of her relationship with Joseph, with Matthew relating that Joseph "took [Mary] as his wife" (1:24) while Luke describes the couple as "engaged" (Luke 2:5). On the other hand, as confusing as it may be in twenty-first-century terms, her youth doesn't necessarily mean Mary was considered a child in her first-century context.

As previously discussed, there isn't a line that definitively marks the transition between childhood and adulthood either in the first-century world or today. However, for girls in the first-century world, the shift from daughter to wife and, soon after, mother represented significant transitions. Thus, when Luke describes Mary as a virgin, or more literally a maiden (Luke 1:27), he wants his readers to understand Mary at the transition point between girlhood and womanhood. The Greek word (*parthenos*) refers to a girl who has gone through puberty and so is physically able to bear a child but who is not yet married and so is not socially ready to take on the role of mother. Put simply, when the angel Gabriel appears to Mary before she becomes pregnant, she is still a child, though because of her engagement she is a child who is already preparing to live into her adult role as wife. But when Mary becomes pregnant, her cultural standing changes. Regardless of whether or not she is married, as one who is about to become a mother, she is identified by her relative Elizabeth as a woman—an adult (1:42). For Matthew, the situation is even more clear, since shortly after learning of her pregnancy, Joseph takes Mary as his wife.

In Luke's story of Jesus' birth, Mary still exists in this liminal space, made more complicated by the possibility discussed above of her enslavement. She is traveling with Joseph, her fiancé, and so is even more clearly identified as one who is about to be married. So, in one sense, Mary is a girl about to become an adult; but in another sense, she can be read as an enslaved girl deprived of her agency, unable, even after giving birth, to claim the same status as a free woman. Add to this that Mary is already "expecting a child," which is a marker of adulthood (2:5), but outside of marriage can lead to ostracization or worse, and Mary's status is fraught with complications.

To add to this, if we assume that Mary was engaged to Joseph at an age typical for young women within her social group, she was probably around fifteen years old at the time—neither at the very youngest moments of childbearing nor at an age that would have been considered old or unusual to remain unmarried.[10] In other words, by age alone, Mary could have been considered either a child or an adult; her pregnancy and impending motherhood, however, suggest that the larger culture would have treated her as an adult, albeit a very new one.

It is historically inaccurate, then, to say that Mary is a child in the story of Jesus' birth. It would not have been culturally unusual for a girl her age to be married or be giving birth. At the same time, as we contemplate the ways in which God is moving and acting among young people, it remains significant to notice that Mary, as an unmarried first-time mother, is still very new to the cultural role of an adult if that is how we understand her. Once when I was reading this passage with teenagers and children in an intergenerational Bible study, several teenagers pointed out that they often feel more comfortable talking about difficult topics with college students and young adults—whom they perceive as better able to relate to their life experiences—than they feel doing so with older adults. They therefore wondered whether the relatively thin line of age and cultural responsibility that distinguishes the shepherds from Mary may have made it easier for the shepherds to approach Mary or even for her to receive the good news that the shepherds proclaimed.

At the same time, as Mary swaddles and cradles her newborn son (2:7), she is living into her new responsibility as a parent. When she receives the proclamation of the shepherds in the early hours after her child's birth, the newness of it all is still fresh. While I recall experiencing joy and wonder at the birth of each of my children, I recollect a particular level of awe and responsibility when, at twenty-five, I cradled our firstborn. I suspect that Mary, as a first-time mother, may herself have been a bit overwhelmed in those first hours and days following Jesus' birth. And so it is no wonder that when Luke tells us that the young shepherds, so close in age and yet increasingly distant in experience, shared the angels' message with her, she "treasured all these words and pondered them in her heart" (2:19). Such pondering is, in its own way, an opportunity for Mary to grow not only in her faith but also in her embodiment of motherhood as she lives into her new role in adult society.

Yet while Mary may be culturally living into her adult role as Jesus' mother (and soon Joseph's wife), there remains something striking that those whose words help her to process this role are themselves children. In the liminal space between childhood and adulthood, the shepherds fit socially and culturally somewhere in the development range between the complete vulnerability of the infant Jesus and the full responsibility that, as an adult, Mary is called upon to bear. Through them, Mary receives a message of hope and responsibility that in this space, they are, perhaps, uniquely suited to bear.

Good News *for* and *by* All People

Even so, the shepherds' message isn't for Mary alone. The angelic message of "good news of great joy for all people" proclaims the birth of a child: Jesus. It is addressed, at least in part, to child shepherds who were tending their flocks alongside their adult counterparts in the Bethlehem fields. And this message is delivered to and treasured by a young woman who is not far from the experiences of childhood herself. While Jesus' birth is certainly good news for all people, this first gospel proclamation seems particularly targeted *to* and *for* (possibly enslaved) children, with adults overhearing and benefiting from it on the sidelines. In a world in which children would have been among the crowds but rarely the targeted audience for most other proclamations, speeches, or oral stories, Luke depicts a stark reversal of roles.

Luke doesn't leave room for confusion over whom the angels' message is intended for either. The shepherds are not simply in the right place at the right time; they are the right people for the right time, and the angelic messengers seek out the shepherds where they know that they will be. The shepherds are with their flocks in the hill country outside of Bethlehem. Although they're in the same region of Jesus' birth—definitely within walking distance in one night—Luke doesn't indicate that they are right next door. In fact, the shepherds make a point of stating that they need to *go* to seek out the newborn about whom they've just been told. Unlike the animals who become impromptu witnesses to Jesus' birth, the shepherds are *chosen* to receive and bear witness to the newborn Savior.

Receiving the Good News

When my host brother Khwezi thought that he had proven my ability to communicate with him in a language he understood, he was positively gleeful. I think that for him this discovery meant that I was more like him—a more recognizable part of his world and community, sharing in his joys and in his struggles. The ability to connect with and communicate with one another is central to human community.

Often, however, such connections are not without their challenges. When our daughter Joanna was two years old, Esther, a member of the church choir, stopped me after worship one day. She told me she was concerned about Joanna's behavior in worship and suggested that I take advantage of the cry room instead. Since including my children in community worship has always been central for me, I immediately bristled at this suggestion, but I managed to thank her for the suggestion and ask what specific behaviors had her concerned. The resulting conversation created the space for Esther and me to get to know one another in a way we hadn't before, and in so doing to truly see each other and the other's concerns.

As it turns out, the behavior in question was my tendency to balance Joanna on the top of the pew in front of us so that she could see the pastor at the altar. The choir sat facing the congregation in worship, and so although our position at the side of the worship space made this unnoticeable to most people, Esther was able to see Joanna balancing quite clearly. She shared that she was a former kindergarten teacher and had seen many children fall from dangerous balancing acts and so was worried Joanna would get hurt. I assured her that I had a solid hold on Joanna and then explained that she wasn't balancing just for fun, but that I wanted her to see and recognize the pastor during Communion and the prayers. By communicating with and understanding one another better, I was able to adapt how I held Joanna slightly to ease Esther's fears, and Esther was able to relax when she saw me holding Joanna. Ultimately, Esther's courage in expressing her concern directly to me allowed us to balance our needs and be able to worship together better.

For the youngest among the Bethlehem shepherds, the mere idea that God had become incarnate as a child, as *one of them*—complete with the dangers and obstacles they routinely endured—represented a similar connection. In Luke's Gospel, hope is embodied for the children among the shepherds in the person of a savior who is like them. The advent of God as an infant is a clear statement of the profound value God holds not only for humanity in general but for children in particular. God has chosen to share in their joys and, perhaps especially, in their vulnerabilities and struggles.

As Christians, we often celebrate God's incarnation in Jesus as proof that God values the humanness of our lives, our very real and embodied experiences of life. We celebrate that God becomes a part of our human world and communities. What can sometimes be missed is that God did not descend to earth as a fully grown embodied adult able to immediately control and navigate these communities. Instead, God chose to be born in the embodied form of an infant who, instead, depends upon the community for protection and support. God chose to experience humanity in all of its vulnerabilities and faults, including those in infancy and childhood—indeed, to be one of us *at our most vulnerable*.

God entered human community as an infant in need of that community for support. There is no question that as a baby Jesus would have required constant care and attention. However, by identifying with children in this way, God doesn't simply make God's self vulnerable, God also ensures that Jesus will be fully incorporated into his human family and their world because of the care that an infant demands. The infant Jesus needs Mary to swaddle and feed him; he needs the shepherds to declare to Mary and Joseph and their larger community the good news of his birth. Even as he is born Savior and Messiah, Jesus is dependent upon the care and action of others. Or more to the point, Jesus, Mary, and the shepherds are dependent upon one another.

Our eldest, Becca, was a newly walking and talking one-year-old as our church began to prepare for what was to be her first experience of a Christmas pageant. Although our congregation didn't have many children, Becca was born around the same time that four-year-old Jonah, one of the most active members of our small Sunday school, welcomed his little brother, Tristan. As we planned for the program, Jonah was convinced that Tristan and Becca would be in the show. So it was soon decided that Jonah's grandmother would sew the toddlers' sheep costumes; Jackie, a middle school youth, volunteered to "shepherd" them in the pageant. Without the toddlers, I suspect, Jackie might have considered herself too old for the production; however, Jackie's presence helped to manage the chaos of toddlers and helped to fill out the small cast of the show. The result not only was some of the most precious pictures from a Christmas pageant that I've ever taken, but a beautiful display of interdependence as, together, the oldest and youngest children cast in the pageant that year enabled one another to participate and find joy and encouragement in one another's presence.

Such interdependency is displayed in sharp relief when we recognize the youth and vulnerability that characterize so many of the characters in the nativity story. By becoming incarnate as a child, God shifts the balance of power. Instead of simply caring for humanity in a one-sided way, God, through Jesus, allows humanity to care for God. In a true testimony to the interdependence of all creation and, indeed, even the Creator, God demonstrates God's own deep-seated need of and dependence upon us.

Khwezi may not have needed me to help with the goats, but he had no problem acknowledging that he needed me and the other adults in his life in other ways. He needed his Ouma to cook for him, he needed Joseph and Nceba to help him learn the harder work on the farm, and he needed me to understand him. And, without a doubt, I needed Khwezi that afternoon, just as Jackie, Tristan, and Becca needed one another in the Christmas program. Bearing witness to and participating in these relationships of mutual care and concern highlights for me the truth that we are in relationship with all of the other people in our individual communities and in the larger world in which we live.

The truth is that we're all connected, and we're all vulnerable. Even as our technology advances, the geopolitical consequences of such advancements illustrate this interconnectedness at a global level. Whether infant or adult, human beings are fragile and vulnerable; we need one another as surely as we need water, shelter, or food. In Luke's Gospel, this is what salvation is about. Salvation is not solely an otherworldly experience in heaven or physical or economic healing in the present; it is an overall experience of wellness that encompasses all of that and more. The Greek word for salvation (*soterion*) literally means to be made well or to be made whole. In its best sense, this is the peace that the angels proclaim. And it's already happening in their midst.

The good news that the shepherds received, therefore, was as immediate and exciting for them as the story was that Khwezi had to share with the rest of his family when they returned home. And as many of them were likely small children themselves, it's little surprise that their enthusiasm was no less intense. Anyone who has spotted the grins on little faces waving streamers in procession in worship, or the proud stance of newly minted acolytes who have successfully completed their duties knows the joy with which children can embrace the tasks to which they are entrusted in worship and service to God.

Even more so, then, is the joy when the good news that the shepherds receive is not a disconnected prophecy removed from their daily lives; it is the promise of a God who, through Jesus, has become an intimate part of their lives, bearing peace and stability that has the potential to change them. As a mixed group of children and adults, all relatively low on the social and economic hierarchies of the Roman world, the Bethlehem shepherds seem a fitting group to receive this message. It would be difficult for them to pretend that they don't need one another or anyone else, including God. Because of their age and economic position, the shepherds are on the opposite end of the Roman power hierarchies; at the same time, leaning into the early manuscripts that prefer to translate this passage "peace among those *whom God favors*" (emphasis added), the shepherds rise to the top of the new social order that Jesus' birth has begun.

God intends the good news of salvation for all people; however, this salvation can only be experienced completely when all people, especially those with privilege or power, lean into the needs of those who have for too long been denied such peace. Maybe this is why

God, who is all powerful, chooses to give up that power and accept human care as an infant. The message is clear: humble yourselves and become like those who are usually treated as the "least." For Luke, this mostly included young children and the economically destitute. Today this list has grown. In the predominantly White Protestant churches I am most actively a part of, children and the poor, while lifted up as communities to serve, continue to be put at the margins of actual worship and service communities. However, such churches also minoritize and exclude many more people due to their racialization, gender, (dis)abilities, and sexuality, among other embodied identities. Even as we strive to "include" or "accept" some members of marginalized communities, most White churches fail to recognize that we need these fellow members of Christ's body just as much as, if not more than, they need us.

Whoever the metaphorical shepherds are in our individual communities, the call of the gospel is to lean into God's favor for those whom the structures of power and privilege would prefer to discount. It is to and for *these beloved* that the good news of Jesus was originally proclaimed. It is by the gift of the original shepherds receiving this good news, of Mary as a young, unwed, enslaved mother caring for her infant son, and of God taking on infant flesh that we have anything at all to proclaim. Receiving this good news, then, means not only reciting the words but recognizing from whom the words come and, for that matter, who they are first about.

In order to live together and celebrate the gospel as a message for all people, we must begin by acknowledging that this message was first given to and received by specific people. Just as Jesus himself was embodied as an infant, the reception and celebration of his birth was first embodied by the closest equivalent the first century had to poor and working-class children. God establishes God's realm not by catering to the preferences of moneyed adults but by coming alongside poor children.

The contemporary activist group Black Lives Matter, itself begun among students—children—has been criticized by White counterprotestors, many of them Christian, who promote the slogan "All lives matter." While in principle correct—all lives should and do matter to God—this criticism can miss the fundamental point that in America today it is primarily Black and Brown lives that are treated as though they don't matter and, therefore, there is a need to explicitly state their value. Similarly Judean, Galilean, and other lives indigenous to the territories Rome conquered were particularly threatened in the Roman Empire of Jesus' day. To help explain this, the counter-slogan "All lives can't matter until Black lives matter" has become popular. In direct refutation of the Roman illusion of universal peace, this seems to be similar to what the angels are saying in Luke: "All people can't experience peace until the shepherds have peace." Or, perhaps even more pointedly, "All people can't experience peace until the little ones whom God favors have peace."

As those who wish to live into God's realm in the contemporary world, we've already seen that this means flipping the tables on whose needs and preferences are considered first—by focusing on welcoming and removing stumbling blocks from God's "little ones." By reconsidering the familiar Christmas story with attention to the peace God desires for these little ones, we can move a step farther and begin the work of removing the stumbling blocks to that peace, which prevent the experience of true peace for all of us. Put differently, making space to hear the shepherds' message can help the Marys and Josephs in our midst to ponder and treasure anew the word of God that God's "little ones" proclaim.

When it comes to actively receiving the gospel, the shepherds demonstrate that this is more than simply reading the gospel or hearing it proclaimed at a Sunday service. The shepherds *embody* the gospel that they receive, not only by their response to Jesus but also by their courage to share the good news with Mary, Joseph, and their whole community. Despite my best efforts to advocate for the full inclusion of children in worship, I would be lying if I didn't admit that when I was worshiping regularly with an infant, a toddler, and a first-grader in tow, there were times I would lament that I spent the entire service wrangling children rather than hearing the sermon or reflecting upon the gospel. But there were other times when one of those children would point to her heart and tell me that's where Jesus was, or plant a kiss on her baby brother to help calm his wiggles; then I knew I was experiencing the gospel, through them, firsthand.

Whatever our age or position in the secular world, we would do well to follow the examples set by these Bethlehem shepherds. The shepherds receive the word that a new child has been born who is already *in that very moment* "the Messiah, the Lord" (Luke 2:11) and who, at the same time and just as remarkably, is a vulnerable child *just like them*. And they do not hesitate to respond. They do not hesitate to accept that this infant child is the incarnation of God's good news—the gospel for them.

These young shepherds did not receive just any message. They didn't receive a generic proclamation of the realm of God or even of God's reversal of wealth and privilege. Each of the shepherds outside of Bethlehem, including the many children in their midst, received an angelic message of good news uniquely intended for them. It was a personal message, an intentional sign, a divine breath of connection. The angelic proclamation of good news was spoken to vulnerable children who were dwelling literally on the outskirts of their small village, calling them into the center of the saving work of God. It was a message of value, to and for the present.

The birth of Jesus is not just good news for the fanciful future, the stuff of precarious hopes; it is good news of a present reality. By bringing God's message of peace to the shepherds, the angels are already turning the Roman definitions of power and favor on their heads. And who better to entrust with the good news of a child who will work salvation than children themselves? As children and those who work closely with children, the shepherds deeply and personally understand both the dangers and promises of childhood. For them, the message that God has come into the human world in the form of a child is received with great joy and appreciation, and this joy is not contained within themselves but is quickly shared with all those they encounter.

Proclaiming the Good News

The Bethlehem shepherds don't stop at receiving or even embodying the good news. Like Khwezi, once they have a message to share, they cannot seem to keep it to themselves. The shepherds aren't solely passive hearers of the gospel message; they're also active proclaimers. I tell the story of Khwezi because he was himself a child shepherd—a reminder that even though we have a tendency to coddle and segregate children in many communities in the United States, this is not the reality, or even the norm, in most of the world. Indeed, even in families where children's roles are limited, attention to their contributions—whether through feeding the family pet, helping cook an evening meal, or even offering their honest reflections on and thoughts on the day, children continue to be vital and integral parts of their families, neighborhoods, and churches. When I attended worship with Khwezi's family during my homestay, our Sunday service consisted of Bible readings and songs beneath a large, shady tree together with neighbors from the communal farmland. As we stood in that shade, every one of us sang together, with the children singing just as loudly and at times with even more enthusiasm than the adults. At the same time, many of those children rode on the shoulders of their fathers or the backs of their mothers for the walk to and from our gathering.

The integration of children into communities and churches does not and should not necessitate the loss of their protections and accommodations as children. As shepherds, those who visited Jesus' family contributed to economic production in Bethlehem, but as children they still required protections and provisions from their families and communities as well. To apply a phrase from preaching professor Richard W. Voelz to the shepherds' more ancient context, proclamation (both then and now) portrays "young people not simply as listeners to, but also as *producers of* preaching."[11] They both brought and received gifts at the foot of the manger.

What the shepherds as producers do with the angelic message is as compelling as, if not more so, the fact that the angels address it to them in the first place. Like the infant Jesus about whom they proclaim, the shepherds are actively involved in the living out of God's good news in their present. Therefore, it isn't surprising that the shepherds accept and proclaim the present promise of Jesus' birth for what it is, without any pause or caveat about its future potential. The shepherds, as typical children, are living in the moment. And in that moment they adapt quickly. Although the shepherds are fearful at first after hearing the angels' message, they quickly come to believe and make haste to go where the angels have sent them (Luke 2:16). This haste is a testament not only to their youthful enthusiasm but also to the natural trust with which that enthusiasm is imbued.

When I read about the shepherds' haste, I'm again reminded of my host brother Khwezi running excitedly to tell his Ouma what he had learned about me while she was away, or more recently of my own children clamoring at the door to tell me the stories of their days with unrivaled focus and enthusiasm, or of the countless children who have proudly presented to me as their pastor a drawing of the day's gospel story while exiting worship. What stands out in these actions isn't just the excitement of their announcements, but the speed and confidence with which they rush to share them. There is never anything more urgent for my seven-year-old son than whatever is on his mind in that moment; and frequently, when I pick them up from school, my two elementary-aged children clamor over each other, unable to wait even for the other to finish telling me about the latest happenings in their days.

Immediately after the angels leave them, the shepherds confer and without hesitation declare, "Let us go now to Bethlehem and see this thing that has taken place, which the Lord has made known to us" (Luke 2:15). I don't know that I've ever witnessed a group of adults decide upon a course of action with such clarity and speed; however, children on playgrounds across the world routinely invent and institute games and report exciting events going on around them with haste. But children do not proclaim *everything* so quickly. If I ask my children to announce bedtime or to gather their siblings for a chore or other activity they aren't interested in doing, their feet can drag at the speed of molasses.

With this view in mind, I've been presenting this story to adult Bible study groups for some time now, noting that the speed with which the shepherds rush to respond to the angelic command is representative of their youth. The adults in these studies have generally agreed with and even reiterated these conclusions; however, when I read this Scripture in an intergenerational study that included children for the first time, the response was radically different. When I asked this intergenerational group to speculate as to how the shepherds' youth may have influenced their response to the angels' message, two boys, around the ages of eight and eleven, immediately replied, "It must have made it harder!" When I asked these boys to describe what they meant, one explained, "As a kid, being told to go find an adult that you've never met before must have been really scary." His friend added, "Sometimes it's scary enough to talk to adults when you know who they are. But Mary and Joseph weren't even *expecting* the shepherds, so they would have had to knock on their door and explain who they were. I think I'd be too scared to talk." And upon thinking about it like that, I had to agree. I'd be scared to knock on the door of a stranger and share an angelic message even as an adult.

So while I still think that the speed with which the shepherds respond to the angelic pronouncement may have been representative of their youthful energy and enthusiasm, I now imagine that halfway to the gates of Bethlehem, at least some of these young shepherds may have had second thoughts. With the reality of the angels' task setting in, they may have begun to wonder whether they could or should go through with it. And yet, remarkably, they did. Whether this is to the credit of one or more courageous and particularly gregarious young shepherds, or a mark of their extreme faith and trust, we cannot know. I suspect that it might have been a bit of both.

Trust is a quality nurtured in adults and children alike over time; it is by no means a guaranteed privilege of childhood. Nonetheless, trust comes more naturally to children. Despite Khwezi's suspicions that I may not have been entirely forthcoming with him in my facility with language, he nonetheless trusted me as a companion to play and laugh with and even to help him with the goats when the situation demanded it. In a similar situation, an adult, I suspect, might have been less forthcoming. When my son William was one year old, he struggled to sit still during worship. Frequently, he would roam up and down the aisles, looking to gather loose pencils or scraps of paper before eventually making his way back to me. One Sunday as he was making his way down the center aisle, a gentleman about six rows back smiled and waved at him. William smiled back and joined that man, Frank, and his family in his pew. I watched as Frank nodded approvingly at my son's cache of pencils, steadied the paper as

William scribbled enthusiastically for a moment or two, and gave him a high five as he went once again on his way. William hadn't formally met or interacted with Frank before, but in the safety of our worship space, where he had known nothing but joy and affirmation, William trusted him implicitly. And in that moment, as a fellow member of the body of Christ, Frank helped to build and nurture William's trust.

Because of their increased dependence and vulnerability, children rely more upon others to survive and are born with a predisposition to trust those who care for them. Children who, like Khwezi and William, have known protection in their homes and communities tend to display a higher level of trust. It is a virtue from which adults can learn, and it is this kind of complete trust that seems to motivate the shepherds' swift movements.

Trust in the God of Israel was taught to Jewish children from birth. The common people in first-century Judea, which would have included shepherds, were almost all Jewish. This religious incorporation of children, combined with an absolute trust in the divine message taught in their synagogues and homes, enables the shepherds, even as children, to receive the angelic message with unwavering trust. They do not debate, question the reality of what they have just experienced, or otherwise delay their departure with any number of concerns that can stall good ministry in its tracks. They simply go, and they go with haste (Luke 2:16).

Throughout the Gospels, the shepherds' response is mirrored by those who respond to the good news Jesus proclaims and who seek to live into God's realm. This can be seen in the *immediate* response of Simon, Andrew, James, and John to Jesus' call (Mark 1:18–20) and in the women's haste in running to tell the others about his empty tomb (Matt. 28:8). At the heart of each of these responses is a childlike trust and an eagerness to make known the good news as each disciple comes to know it. Rather than fretting about how best *we* can hear God's word, the shepherds remind us that those who have truly received this word cannot keep it to themselves any more than a little child bubbling over with an exciting secret or revelation.

And so it should not be surprising that these faithful young shepherds are the ones who reveal to Mary and Joseph the extent of what has taken place that night with the birth of their son (Luke 2:19). Nor is it surprising that after visiting Jesus' family the shepherds return through the city proclaiming the angels' message widely as they go, "glorifying and praising God" (2:20). These two acts are incredible moments of proclamation from which we can all learn.

By making known all that they had been told, the shepherds show themselves not only to be trusting but also to be trustworthy and reliable communicators. As any good sermon should, the shepherds' message inspires Mary. Although Mary has already had her own angelic pronouncement (Luke 1:26–38), she not only treasures the shepherds' words but "ponder[s] them in her heart" (2:19). Their proclamation provokes faith and further reflection in Mary, who will continue to care for Jesus and, in her own way, help to bring about the good news of the promises proclaimed.

In this way, the shepherds make no pretense that their proclamation is an end in itself. They don't seem to expect that their word is the end of the story—indeed, with the savior they proclaim still a newborn infant, how could they? Yet neither do they downplay the significance of their good news. The shepherds model for us a form of proclamation that might better be understood as participation in a holy conversation. Rather than assume that any one party has a monopoly on God's revelation, everyone in the stable seems to have something to offer to one another. The shepherds are eager to experience the good news embodied in the Christ child, and Mary treasures what they have to say.

Although Luke doesn't record the specifics of any conversation, I suspect that in that holy moment, the shepherds and Mary shared together about the great things that God was doing in their midst. Even if Mary remained silent, the depth of her trust and obedience to God was embodied as she cared for her infant. Mary, the shepherds, and even Jesus trust and therefore bless and enrich one another. Again, the power structures of the Roman world that insisted all authority be invested in one person were beginning to crumble.

The shepherds' message is not just reserved for Mary and Joseph, who (Mary at least) have already experienced their own epiphanies, but quickly spreads to *all who heard* (Luke 2:18). While it is unclear who else may be present at this point, the busyness of Bethlehem suggested in Luke 2:7 makes it unlikely that the family is alone. And even if they are alone, Mary and Joseph do not keep the shepherds' words a secret.

The shepherds "made known what had been told them about this child" (Luke 2:17), presumably to a larger crowd that has now gathered around since the infant's birth. Apart from the description of Mary's personal reaction, Luke tells us that "all [in Greek, *pantes*] who heard [the shepherds' proclamation] were amazed" (2:18). This expansive "all" seems to reach beyond just Mary and Joseph and suggests that even before the shepherds leave the stable, the good news that they've heard and shared is beginning to spread.

While the shepherds are highlighted as the first proclaimers of the good news of Jesus' birth, it's unlikely that the message stopped with them. Just as they received the angels' message and immediately shared it with others, so too their message may have been shared more broadly by those who heard their proclamation and were amazed. Perhaps word of the shepherds' proclamation is what alerted Anna and Simeon to watch for a special child to be brought to Jerusalem (see Luke 2:27–38), or formed the bedtime stories Mary and Joseph shared with Jesus as a child. If Luke's account is reliable, someone remembered and passed on these events to the evangelist so that he could write them down. Whatever the case, the focus isn't on who has the correct or authoritative teaching, but on a communal excitement for and an embrace of the peace that comes from Jesus as a newborn savior.

My colleague Ronald Allen advocates for a kind of collaborative preaching that he terms "roundtable" preaching—a proclamation of the message that neither begins nor ends with the preacher but is a shared experience for all involved. The idea is to invite everyone into the experience of receiving, pondering, embodying, and proclaiming the good news. The authority figure of the preacher sometimes makes it difficult for other congregants to fully live into this conversation. For some this may come from shyness about talking about God with others, or a fear that our interpretation might be the "wrong" interpretation, or a paralysis around where and how to start. The Gospels give us our fair share of "failed" proclamation stories to support such fears of speaking out. The women who witness the empty tomb in Mark's Gospel are so frightened that Mark tells us "they said nothing to anyone" (Mark 16:8). And even when other Gospel accounts describe the women as going on to share the good news, most of the male disciples ignore them (Luke 24:11), and those who do listen insist on going to see for themselves (Luke 24:12; John 20:2). Especially for those who are not empowered by traditional structures, moving from receiving to proclaiming the gospel can be frightening.

However, the shepherds' experience offers an encouraging contrast to the reception of the women who proclaimed the empty tomb. The shepherds' recitation of their angelic revelation inspires "amazement" rather than scorn and doubt among all who heard them. Indeed, although Mark's Gospel ends with Mary Magdalene, Mary the mother of James, and Salome silent in fear, the very fact that the good news of Jesus' resurrection has been told across the centuries—and that the women are a part of it—confirms that they did not remain silent forever. And just as in John's account Peter and the Beloved Disciple eventually ran to confirm Mary's words, so have generations found hope and peace in the good news that these women proclaimed. Who knows, perhaps one of the unnamed women who proclaimed the empty tomb was even a Bethlehem shepherdess who proclaimed the Messiah's birth. The implicit ending of the Gospel story, then, is ultimately one that parallels Luke's beginning—the good news being shared by the least-expected witnesses, embraced and expanded in a roundtable of proclamation.

Children may be the first to proclaim the good news of Jesus, but they are not the last. Likewise, women may be the first to proclaim Christ's resurrection, but this proclamation is only the beginning. By sharing the good news without pretense or assumption, something children seem particularly adept at doing, the shepherds produce a model for proclamation that relies on community rather than hierarchy—on collaboration rather than authority. Just as importantly, by receiving the shepherds' proclamation with wonder and awe, Mary participates in and extends their message. If we identify Jesus' mother as one of the Marys who discovered the empty tomb—as tradition often does—then it is easy to see how this later proclamation would have been grounded in the young mother's embrace of the first gospel message.

It is this kind of roundtable preaching that best embodies the interdependent nature of the church as the body of Christ. What I learned from my experience with Khwezi is the importance of appreciating each person, no matter how young, and respecting their abilities. Khwezi was, of course, still a child. Had I not been present, I don't know whether his family would have left him at home on his own. Certainly, once we came in from the storm, Khwezi seemed to want, if not need, my companionship. And yet while respecting his needs as a child, his family also took Khwezi seriously for the ways in which, as a child, he was able to contribute to the family farm.

To say that children in agricultural communities, both past and present, work to contribute to the family's well-being doesn't mean that they are not still children in need of nurture, protection, and support. When Khwezi's Ouma returned, Khwezi was as excited as I was to receive the treat of fruit punch mixed in water to enjoy on the hot day. He needed the reassurance and affirmation of his family. He also complained bitterly to Ouma that I had refused to speak with him, even though he insisted that I could "clearly" understand Afrikaans. As adept as he was at caring for the goats and his errant teenage host sister, Khwezi still needed his grandmother. And although that day I needed Khwezi more than he needed me, the truth is we needed one another.

The same is true in the experience of proclamation. Children producing a Christmas pageant have the potential to share the good news of Jesus's birth in powerful, compelling ways. However, they need the respect and support of their teachers, directors, ministers, and audience. Likewise, there are other times when it is more appropriate for children to listen to the good news of the gospel that these same individuals proclaim to them. This is the homiletical circle, or roundtable, that Allen talks about.

In a family or in a church, one person's strengths complement another's weaknesses. The point in celebrating the shepherds' proclamation as an act of preaching performed by children is not to romanticize the words of children or regard them as a source of entertainment. It certainly isn't to create a religious edition of "Kids Say the Darndest Things." Instead, it is to recognize the gifts of insight that we can share with one another. It is to truly listen to—pondering, treasuring, and proclaiming—the words that the "little ones" in our midst share. And in so doing, it is to embody the kind of trust that empowers young children to excel.

Whether they are relegated to the supporting role in children's pageants or human scenery in scholarly articles, the shepherds of Luke's infancy narrative are often neglected for their particular place within Luke's larger narrative and for their contribution to the advent of God's realm, which the birth of Jesus begins. The shepherds become one more example of Luke's great message of reversal revealed through Jesus. However, when we add to this an appreciation for the children likely to have been present among these Bethlehem shepherds, their contribution to the broader narrative whole is highlighted, and we can begin to appreciate them not only for what they did but for who they are.

But it isn't just the shepherds who display trust when they rush to share the good news. The angels themselves must first entrust this news to the shepherds. In the analogy of a roundtable conversation, the angels pull up a chair and invite the young and impoverished to the table. And then, even more remarkably, they set down their prepared notes and glorious hymns and leave the shepherds to carry the proclamation forward. They invite action and then leave the next steps to those gathered with them. God trusts the shepherds to continue the conversation. The first sermon about Jesus the Messiah is not complete when the angels disappear. It is just beginning. And it is the young shepherds, responding in haste, who carry the next chords.

The good news of the shepherds' story isn't just that God saw fit to reveal God's inbreaking realm to these ordinary working children, but that upon revealing God's self, God saw fit to entrust these same children with carrying forward the message. The question for the church today is this: Can we do the same? Can we entrust the message of the gospel to the mouths of children? And can we then take seriously and ponder what it is that they have to say?

The shepherds of Luke's nativity shine as proclaimers of the gospel who are experiencing the glory of the infant Jesus in its immediacy. Their message is received with trust and amazement and inspires others in the living out of God's realm, even as they continue out this same agenda in the praise and glorification they give. What is perhaps most striking about my Namibian host family is that they took the time to listen to Khwezi when he shared what had happened to us that day, and when Khwezi finished regaling them with his tale of how their American visitor most certainly must speak Afrikaans, nobody shamed him for getting the details wrong, even as they laughed. In fact, everybody believed that most of the story Khwezi told was the truth, even though he misinterpreted the meaning of some of it. Although my host family was amused by Khwezi's confusion, they engaged with him and encouraged him.

Unfortunately, when children like Khwezi tell their truths in church communities, whether at children's time or Sunday school or over the fellowship hour, few adults pause to take them so seriously. Indeed, it has become easier in some instances for many Christians to laugh at what the youngest members of Christ's body have to say than to ponder, as Mary did, with wonder and awe at the meaning behind it. Yet living in community together, being a part of a family together, as Christ calls the Christian body to do, requires fuller support and love. It beckons us to attend a children's Christmas pageant not in search of cute costumes or humorous "outtakes," but rather with expectance that the Word of God will be revealed to us anew. Living in Christian community demands that the same respect adult members ask of the children be given to the children as well. For the body of Christ thrives on the ability to truly hear, receive, and ponder the words of one another—both child and adult.

For Further Reading

Allen, Ronald J., and O. Wesley Allen Jr. *The Sermon without End: A Conversational Approach to Preaching*. Nashville: Abingdon, 2015.

Crowder, Stephanie Buckhanon. "Mary: A Favor(less) Mother (Luke 1:26–38)." In *When Momma Speaks: The Bible and Motherhood from a Womanist Perspective*. Louisville, KY: Westminster John Knox, 2016.

Horsley, Richard A. *The Liberation of Christmas: The Infancy Narratives in Social Context*. Eugene, OR: Wipf and Stock, 1989.

Lindeman Allen, Amy. "A Sign for You: A Child Savior Revealed to Child Shepherds." *Biblical Interpretation* 29, no. 2 (2021): 229–255.
Voelz, Richard W. *Youthful Preaching*. Eugene, OR: Cascade, 2016.

Questions for Discussion

1. Recall a time as a child when you were bursting with excitement to share some sort of news, or when a child has come to you in a similar way. What did it feel like? How did you and those around you respond?
2. Recall a time when as a child or an adult you were hesitant to share good news. What caused your hesitation? How did you feel? Did you ultimately share the good news? If so, who or what helped you find the strength and courage to share your news?
3. We are all called to proclaim the good news of Jesus in a general sense, but in what specific way is God calling you to add to the proclamation in your present time and place?
4. What is the good news that the children in your life (your family, your congregation, your community) need to hear right now?
5. Children can often be excited to share what's on their mind, but adults are not always so eager to listen. Who are the children who are speaking (or trying to speak) to you? What are they saying? How can you listen better?

Chapter Three

The Gift of Advocacy

Fisherfolk

> "Follow me and I will make you fish for people."
> —Mark 1:17

Noah and Natalie live in a suburban community outside of Indianapolis. As fifth-graders, this brother and sister were learning leadership and community skills together with the rest of their peers in school. As the oldest students in the school, fifth-graders are the "upperclassmen" and natural leaders. Fifth-graders earn special privileges, such as the ability to shop in the students' rewards store and to volunteer with school services. At the same time, this is a time in which teachers help students to plan for their transition into middle school, to select an instrument to learn in sixth grade, to transition between classes by subject area, and to hone their math and writing skills. In short, these students are learning to connect with a continually growing community.

The fifth- and sixth-grade Sunday school class that Noah and Natalie attended at Good Samaritan Church, called the "Explorer" class, was designed to help students build these same skills from a faith perspective. This group of children met weekly after worship to talk about their faith as it relates to their lives in school, family, and community. At an age in which children are continuing to think more and more beyond their own selves and family to connect with the wider community, this class encouraged critical thinking about how Christian Scriptures call us to do just that.

One of the gifts of this particular class is that both the children and their adult leaders were encouraged to bring current events into their weekly conversations and to think about these events in relation to their faith. Such a model empowers the children to feel a part of their own learning as well as to pay attention to and engage with what is going on in their community and beyond. Over the course of Noah and Natalie's fifth-grade year, the class had conversations ranging from love of neighbor to active anti-racism. So when there was local controversy around a proposal for an Islamic seminary and planned housing development in their community, it's not surprising that the Explorer class talked about it.

The Sunday school teacher explained the proposal that was going to be sent to the county commissioners and shared that, in advance of this proposal, there had been vocal community concern expressed by some adults in the community against this development. In social media forums and in public letters and comments to the county commissioners, these adults expressed concern that the call to prayer would be too loud and that an intentionally Muslim development ("only for their people") would negatively impact property values for the predominantly White Christians already living in the area.

The Explorer class discussed these concerns and the potential positives that an Islamic mosque, seminary, and housing development would bring to their community. In the end, the children in this class decided that they wanted to write a letter to the county commissioners to be read alongside other community comments. This is what they wrote:

> To the Hendricks County Commissioners,
>
> We are a group of fifth- and sixth-grade students in the Explorers class at Good Samaritan Church. We talked about the John Phillip Villages development, and we wanted to share our thoughts about this development.
>
> We think it would be a great asset to our community. Having this could open our eyes and could help us build bridges to

> different cultures, which is good because it's nice to have more cultures and to learn more about different cultures.
>
> We know that one of the claims against the mosque being built is that it will expose children to a different religion. But as children in our community ourselves, we think that it is a good thing to learn about our differences and that not everyone is a white Christian. The more diversity that exists in our lives, the richer our lives might be.
>
> We have heard that some people have been mean to the people who would move into the planned Muslim community. We don't understand this. Maybe it is because some Christians in our county are afraid of Muslims. We want you know that most Muslims are good and peaceful people.
>
> Thank you for considering our thoughts and words as students in our community. Our town is a growing community, and we cannot deny, resist, or stop change.

Unfortunately, the commissioners listened to the outpouring of adult voices against this development more closely than they listened to the children. The development was unanimously voted down, even after it had been provisionally recommended in an earlier meeting. The vitriol over this community only grew with time, and when Noah joined his father a year later to speak in favor of the development in a different community site at a later county commissioners meeting, they witnessed an Islamic boy who was speaking about what this community would mean for him and his family publicly booed by adults sitting in the gallery.

While the letter from the Explorer Sunday school class did not ultimately change the political decision, it did enable the children to make their voices heard as a part of their larger community. Their letter was read both in public comment at the county commissioners meeting and in the church announcements at worship ahead of that meeting. Their words inspired several adults from their congregation to get involved and speak up at the county commissioners meeting too. The passion and commitment of such young people reminds us that children are not our "future." They are a part of our present. Young people are as deeply, if not more deeply, impacted by so much of what goes on in our neighborhoods and our world, even if, as adults, we may sometimes forget to ask them how they are experiencing any of it.

Fisherfolk

Matthew 4:18–22; Mark 1:16–34; Luke 5:1–11

The same desire to claim agency and leadership nurtured in the Explorer Sunday school class existed in the first-century world too. Just as young people like Noah and Natalie found their voices in speaking up for neighbors in their community, even amid adult objections, so too children in the crowds Jesus preached to were inspired to use their voices for the sake of loving their neighbors and improving their communities. The inclusion of youth as integral parts of the larger community in both of these contexts made it possible for them to press the boundaries of those communities when needed. Indeed, there is no reason to imagine that youth and children were not a part of the many who followed Jesus from Galilee to Jerusalem, whom both Mark and Luke describe as disciples.

When most people picture Jesus' disciples, they're usually thinking about the Twelve, but those aren't the only ones to have followed and supported Jesus in his ministry.[1] Scripture suggests that the actual group was much larger than this, numbering more than seventy, including many who followed Jesus all the way from his beginnings in Galilee. Close attention to the dynamics of the first-century world has already helped us to see that youth and children were among these larger groups, perhaps often in ways similar to Noah's attendance at the county commissioners meeting with his father.

But we need not think of the children among Jesus' disciples as simply a part of the crowd. Especially for the older children in these groups, there was a growing sense of community involvement and leadership. Therefore, it's worth considering whether it's possible for there to have been children among the leaders of Jesus' disciples—the Twelve. The list of their names varies slightly in the Gospel accounts, but the main characters are the same: there's Judas Iscariot, the disciple who betrayed Jesus; Simon, the informal spokesperson for the Twelve and the one whom Jesus nicknamed Peter, "the rock"; and Peter's brother, Andrew.[2]

Also consistent across each list is a second pair of brothers, James and John, the sons of Zebedee. These brothers share their call story with Peter and Andrew, who are fishing together on the Sea of Galilee when Jesus first calls them to "fish for people" (Mark 1:17). Collectively, the response of these brothers is remembered as the first and perhaps most famous response to Jesus' summons. Later, Peter, James, and John form an informal inner group of those who witness Jesus' power in ways in which not all the chosen Twelve are always privy. They are, in short, the leaders among the leaders. Together these three join Jesus to witness healings, teachings, and even the transfiguration of Jesus upon a mountaintop.

But first, they are fishers. (Although the NRSV uses the term "fishermen," I prefer "fishers" because it more clearly denotes the profession without assuming any particular age or generation and as such is a more accurate translation of the original Greek text.) Simon, Andrew, James, and John live in the same coastal town of Galilee (probably Capernaum) and work together in a fishing cooperative to help feed and support their families. Although these four also seem to have a relationship with one another outside of fishing, evidenced by the presence of James and John at Simon's home (Mark 1:29), Luke tells us that they and their fathers are fishing partners (Luke 5:7). The Greek word *metochos* is a technical term that describes partners in a business arrangement.

Such an arrangement was common in the first-century fishing industry. In such partnerships, families pooled together to share supplies such as boats and nets, oversee the business of catching fish, prepare them for sale (either fresh or, in many cases, salted), and share the profits. They also helped one another with large catches, as described in Luke's account. Matthew and Mark don't name this partnership specifically, but they do describe the pairs working near one another on the Galilean seashore in a way that would have been consistent with such a partnership. The use of plural pronouns and the mention of hired hands in Mark 1:20 also suggest that there were more fishers, perhaps both hired hands and other family members, working together in these boats. Such would have been typical of a fishing cooperative. This kind of organized fishing means that the two pairs of brothers are not simply out on a fishing holiday, nor are they intent on catching just a fish or two for that night's dinner; rather, they are engaged in an organized and likely profitable business. And it is this business, in addition to their supplies and their father, that they leave behind.

It's impossible to know how much of Jesus' message these brothers or those with them knew before that afternoon when Jesus called and they followed. Mark tells us only that Jesus had come to Galilee "proclaiming the good news of God" (Mark 1:14), and then, as he passed along the sea, he called out to these fishers, and they immediately followed (1:16–18). Since Mark's whole Gospel account moves quickly, it is difficult to know whether these verses are minutes or days apart from one another, and so whether the brothers would have been familiar with the good news Jesus proclaimed or whether this would have been their first exposure to it.

Matthew assumes that the brothers would have had a bit more exposure to Jesus' message, and he fills in the gap between the beginning of Jesus' proclamation and his afternoon walk along the seashore by describing Jesus as having made his home in Capernaum, by the Sea of Galilee, and proclaiming that "the kingdom of heaven has come" (Matt. 4:13).[3] By living in this small fishing town, the assumed hometown of the fishers in question, Jesus would likely have known and encountered them before the recorded moment when he calls out to them. The fishers would thus have had the opportunity to hear and consider Jesus' message about God's realm and perhaps even discussed possibilities of working with Jesus prior to this moment of his actual calling and their response (Matt. 4:17–20).

This certainly seems to be the assumption in Luke's Gospel, which places this call story later in the narrative, after Simon, and perhaps the others, have heard Jesus teach in the synagogue (Luke 4:31–37) and witnessed him healing Simon's mother-in-law and many others in his home (4:38–41). Indeed, confirming the divine nature of Jesus' calling, Luke's Jesus does not simply call to the fishers; rather, he first aids them in a miraculous catch of fish and then calls them to follow him, promising them that "from now on you will be catching people" (5:1–11).

Recent translations have shifted the object of this fishing from "men" (KJV, RSV) to "people" (NRSV, NIV), better reflecting the more neutral word *anthrōpōn* in the original Greek. While most may immediately recognize this as a move toward gender inclusivity, gender isn't the only inclusion that the broader translation allows. While "men" refers only to grown males, "people" includes human beings of all genders and ages—the totality of those created in the image of God. Moreover, such inclusivity better reflects the original intent of the Greek, which uses this inclusive term for humanity—the very same word used to describe God's creation of humankind in the Greek translation of Genesis 1:26. The call to discipleship, then, is inclusive.

Luke's telling of the encounter gives these first disciples the greatest opportunity for discernment before leaving everything and following Jesus; however, each Gospel account sets a scene in which the disciples likely had some knowledge of Jesus and his message before answering his call.

Even with such foreknowledge, though, when Jesus finally issues the call to follow, the response of all four fishers in each Gospel is definitive. Matthew and Mark describe the disciples' response as immediate. Simon and Andrew leave behind the nets they have been casting (Matt. 4:20; Mark 1:18). James and John leave their father (Matt. 4:22; Mark 1:20). These two pairs of brothers tangibly demonstrate Jesus' call to leave "everything"—possessions and family—for the sake of the gospel (Mark 10:28–31). Luke summarizes this, indicating that these fisherfolk "left everything and followed him" (Luke 5:11).

In each telling, the message is clear—these fishers follow Jesus eagerly, aware of the good news of the inbreaking realm of God that he has been proclaiming, even if they do not understand the full implications of that proclamation yet.

Children in the Story

Child and Teen Fishers

It's not uncommon today to see children out fishing with their parents or grandparents. (Despite my aversion for worms or any wriggly, slimy things, I owned a Barbie fishing rod once upon a time.) However, most urban Americans would not expect to find many, if any, children on a commercial fishing boat. When we talk about fishing in the first-century world as a livelihood or even a business enterprise, the image we typically associate with the fishers among the disciples—both the Twelve and the others who followed or assisted Jesus along the way—is that of adults.

However, as the previous chapter has shown, first-century children were not as meticulously separated from the work of their families and households as those of many Western children today. Not only were there no child labor laws in the first-century Roman Empire, but child labor was essential to the functioning of the economy. Although a few households may have been privileged enough for the children to devote most of their time to education and leisure, the majority of families struggled each day simply to earn enough money to survive. In these families, every hand counted when it came to completing the day's work, and it was common for children to work alongside of the rest of their family to provide for the household.

The expectation that children participate in the well-being of their household isn't something that has gone away. Many wealthy urban and suburban parents still ask their children to participate in chores, not out of necessity but out of a desire to build skills and character. Moreover, although there are now more protections in place, in many rural parts of the world—both in the United States and across the globe—child participation in agricultural activities such as animal care and fishing remains widespread. The greatest disconnects between imagining a child on a commercial fishing boat don't come from an assumption that children shouldn't participate in the well-being of their family, but from the industrialization that has made many activities—fishing included—larger in scale and more dangerous than they would have been in the preindustrial world of first-century Galilee.

Historians know that small children in first-century Galilee helped with various chores and the herding of small animals, as we have already seen in the story of the shepherds. By the time that these same children reached seven years of age, free boys would begin working alongside their fathers to learn the family trade, and enslaved children would work together with their parents to meet the demands of their household.

In most cases, this is the work that they would have been expected to continue for the rest of their lives. For this reason, it's possible to speculate that the fishers on the Sea of Galilee could have ranged anywhere between seven and seventy years of age—boys learning and practicing their family trade alongside their fathers and grandfathers. Although most of early learning happens in elementary schools today, and math and grammar lessons have largely replaced on-the-job training, the boys learning the fishing trade alongside their fathers would have been just as natural a sight in first-century Galilee as fifth-graders working with teachers to prepare for middle school is in the United States today. Adult biases in translating the Bible, though, led to inserting into the NRSV translation of the Greek word *misthoton* (literally "hired laborers," Mark 1:20) an age category that doesn't exist in the original text, calling these fishers "hired men."

This (mis)translation stems from the assumption that professional fishers would have been full-grown men. But evidence from the Greco-Roman period suggests otherwise. Boys and teenagers worked alongside their elders in the fishing industry. This can be seen in Roman artwork, especially mosaics, that depict boys with no facial hair wearing the haircut and togas of childhood and participating in commercial fishing. In some mosaics, youth are depicted together with older males casting a net from a fishing boat. What is remarkable across the visual representations of Mediterranean fishing in the Roman world is the complete ordinariness with which these works of art depict the inclusion of children in the work of fishing. Combined with the general expectation that children participated in their family trade from a young age, material evidence makes it clear that fishing was a mixed-generation industry.

While this business wasn't commercial in the way we might think of large fishing industries today, it's important to remember that these fishers weren't simply out on a family fishing trip. Fishing in the first century, especially in coastal towns like Galilee, was an organized business and, in most cases, necessary in order to feed one's family and pay for whatever other expenses a household might incur, whether one was a member of one of the partner families or a hired hand. Moreover, while there is little evidence to suggest that enslaved persons were common in such fishing cooperatives, the reality of slavery in the first century leaves reason to believe that some of the household members or hired hands may have been enslaved—including the youth among them.

In short, the laborers who surrounded Simon, Andrew, James, and John in their fishing boats would have included a multigenerational collection of boys and men, some from their own extended families and households, and others from the community at large. Many would have been working under conditions of relative freedom to contribute to their families, while some may have been forced to do so. In truth, in workaday families such as the disciples', even those who were free would not have had much choice in the matter (though, as the Gospels indicate, the freedom to leave did still remain for them).

Among those working on these Galilean fishing boats, teenagers and young adults would largely have been doing the heaviest lifting—pulling in the full-to-overflowing nets of fish. With each person contributing what they could to the business, those at the cusp of adulthood offered the strength and endurance of youth. While there were certainly younger boys and older men, the teens and young men would have provided an essential service to the shared work.

James and John as Teenagers?

Although hired fishers were sometimes needed to supplement the work of Mediterranean fishing cooperatives, the backbone of these smaller cooperatives was typically drawn from one's own household—sons, nephews, grandsons, and, in the first-century economy, enslaved workers. In the case of Zebedee's family, it would not have been unusual for his sons, as soon as they were physically capable, to begin learning this family trade.

We know that the sons of Zebedee were fishers. Moreover, the text suggests that they engaged in fishing not as a hobby but as a professional means to earn a living. From there, as adult (or adult-trained) readers, we typically jump to the conclusion that as professional fishers, the sons of Zebedee were themselves adults. But what if they weren't?

Here we can return to the text for clues as to how the four brothers whom Jesus calls fit into their larger context. The New Testament doesn't give a precise age for any of Jesus' twelve core disciples, or even for Jesus himself. But context clues make it clear that Jesus is an adult when he begins his ministry. Likewise, Luke's Gospel portrays Simon (later called Peter) as an adult. Luke describes Simon as owning his own fishing boat and working among the strongest fishers responsible for pulling in the nets of fish. While his partners James and John are mentioned as the sons of Zebedee, no father is mentioned in relation to Simon, suggesting that he is the head of his household. Moreover, Simon seems to hold a leadership position, perhaps alongside Zebedee, in the fishing cooperative. He is the one with whom Jesus most directly interacts and whose signals others obey. Given the hierarchy explicit both in their society at large and fishing cooperatives in particular, such positions of power and authority would not commonly have been bestowed upon a youth or child.

In addition, Mark's Gospel relates that Simon is married and that he and Andrew share a home where Simon seems to be in control (Mark 1:29–30). Here again Simon is portrayed in a role characteristic of a "head of household" (*pater familias*) who held substantial power within the patriarchal households of the first-century Greco-Roman world. In this culture, no matter how old a man might be, he remained accountable to his father as the head of the household until his father, or for that matter, grandfather, died. Whereas Zebedee remains the head of the household to which James and John belong, Simon, a younger man with the strength to pull in nets, appears to hold this role in his household. Less is known about Simon's brother Andrew, so it is possible that he may have been a minor living in Simon's household. But there is little evidence for this, while the parallel way in which the brothers are described by Mark and Matthew might suggest they are to be understood as close peers. Together with Simon, Mark describes Andrew leaving behind their nets, with a plural possessive, to follow Jesus. In this way, these brothers relinquish the more mature status of householders, leaving behind their power over items of property and business when they abandon their nets, the tools of their trade, at Jesus' calling.

On the other hand, while James and John are also working with nets, Mark highlights neither the nets nor the boat but rather their father as the one whom these brothers leave behind (Mark 1:20). Their father is and remains the head of their household, and so it makes sense that they are not said to abandon their nets, since the nets do not yet belong to them. In both Roman and Jewish tradition, the oldest living male relative remains the head of household throughout his life. Therefore, the presence of Zebedee as a member of an older generation doesn't necessarily mean that James and John are not themselves adults. Average life expectancies, especially among men, made it common for many men to lose their fathers when they were still young. But at the very least, Zebedee's presence, especially as a working member of the fishing cooperative, suggests that these brothers would have been at most young adults, similar in age to Simon and Andrew. In this case, while Simon and Andrew's father seems to have died, leaving Simon in charge of his household and portion of the fishing cooperative, James and John remain under the authority of their father. Sociologists call this the "intermediate generation," referring to adults who have both living children and parents. We know at least that this generational status applied to Simon, who was married (Luke 4:38) and to whom later tradition ascribes at least one daughter, Petronilla (see *Acts of Peter*). Marriage in this time period assumed children as the ideal and Scripture itself suggests that some of Jesus' disciples had children (Matt. 19:27–30; 1 Cor. 9:5)—children who, at least in some cases, are abandoned and put at risk on account of their fathers' discipleship, a point worthy both in Jesus' time and today, of sharp critique.

But we need not assume that every child connected with Jesus' disciples was abandoned. Some may have joined their parents in following Jesus and others may have even turned the tables, abandoning their parents to follow Jesus (see again Matt. 19:27–30). The Gospels at least hint at the possibility that James and John may have been younger than Simon or Andrew due to their living father, perhaps as young as seven years old. In this case, they would be members of the youngest generation, still children themselves—when they first responded to Jesus' call.

That God calls children to God's purpose is attested all the way back to the biblical prophets themselves (see Jer. 1:4–10; 1 Sam. 1–3). Although none of the Gospels are as direct as the prophetic narratives in labeling James or John as children, it's worth noticing that these brothers, uniquely among the disciples, are frequently associated with their family. They are referred to repeatedly as the sons of Zebedee, sometimes without even referencing their given names (Matt. 10:2; Mark 3:17; John 21:2).

Matthew even describes the mother of James and John as joining them in following Jesus and asking Jesus to allow her sons to sit at his right and left hands in God's realm (Matt. 20:20). In this way, she is acting very much in line with a first-century Jewish mother, or really most mothers still today, in seeking the well-being and welfare of her sons. One might imagine that, like Mary, the wife of Zebedee had concerns when her sons left a stable trade to follow an itinerant preacher (Matt. 12:46; Mark 3:31–34). But shrewdly, this mother embraces her sons' course and seeks to secure them the best possible outcome within it.

Mark portrays the same scene but with the brothers themselves approaching Jesus with their request (Mark 10:35). This is perhaps emblematic of the brashness of their youth, since Mark elsewhere nicknames this pair "Sons of Thunder" (3:17). Within the Greco-Roman culture, youth was often characterized as impetuous, active, hot-headed, willful, or headstrong. The adult bias that scorns youthful exuberance comes across here, but underlying it is a truth about the energy many youth bring to engagement with the communities in which they are beginning to come into their own. Although the contexts are very different, the group mocking the Islamic youth who spoke up for his community is not so different from the common dismissal of James and John's enthusiasm as youthful brashness.

Such exuberance, however, stands out more positively in the exercise of strength and stamina necessary to work in fishing boats. For example, the Greek author Aelian highlights the role of youth in manning the nets of fishing boats, in contrast to the older men who may own or maintain the boats.[4] Again, such strength, stamina, and—I would add—optimism continues to resonate today. It certainly fits with the roles James and John play in Zebedee's fishing boat across the Gospel account. In Mark's narrative, they are described as the ones mending the nets (Mark 1:19); in Luke, the only Gospel to recount the actual act of fishing, James and John seem to be among the group of partners who are called to help Simon and Andrew haul in their large catch of fish (Luke 5:7–11).

At the same time, this scene in Luke's Gospel also suggests the youth of James and John through their relative place within the fishing partnership. In ancient Greek there are multiple words that can express collaboration. The first word that Luke uses, *metóchoi* (Luke 5:7), indicates a more formalized business partnership, such as the kinds of fishing cooperatives described above. In contrast, when Luke finally singles out James and John from among the others in their father's boat, he refers to them simply as *koinōnoi* (5:10), a more general term reflecting closeness within a community. While it's true that the four brothers seem to have been a part of the same fishing cooperative, the English translation of both terms as "partner" blurs the distinction between James and John as associates of Simon's and falsely presents James and John as equals in responsibility to their father Zebedee, Simon's more established business partner.

Such descriptions of James and John, together with their descriptions in relation to their family and to their father's fishing business, create a picture in which it is possible to imagine them as boys who, either together with their mother or on their own (and later followed by their mother), decide to follow Jesus as disciples. As in the example of the Explorer Sunday school class, who inspired adult members of their congregation to join them in their advocacy, sometimes—and perhaps most powerfully—youth are able to encourage and lead adults in the right way. For James and John, perhaps it is even their youthful exuberance that enables them to follow Jesus and later, free from the inhibitions and cautions of full adulthood, places them at the center of Jesus' discipleship circle and ultimately inspires their mother to join in the mission.

Yet at the same time, this decision is not without risk. Children can be hurt when they put themselves at the front of the cause, whether from vocal abuse from those who disagree with them, the disappointment that comes when they aren't met with immediate success, or, as in the case of youth political movements against oppressive governments, like the Soweto uprising in apartheid-era South Africa, sometimes much worse. In their social context, James and John may have experienced disapproval and potentially permanent disassociation from their father and his household on account of following Jesus. With this, they may also have lost the future ability to provide for themselves by partnering with their father's fishing cooperative. (Such losses can be seen, for example, in Jesus' parable of the two sons in Luke 18:11–32).

Both Roman and Jewish law would have expected James and John to obey their father as the *pater familias*. Basic to their Jewish family structure, the Ten Commandments exhort children, "Honor your father and your mother, so that your days may be long in the land that the Lord your God is giving you" (Exod. 20:12). Social welfare was based largely upon such family support systems; when Zebedee was no longer able to fish, it was expected that his sons would provide for him. To abandon this obligation meant much more than the material losses that all four brothers might have suffered by walking away from the instruments of their fishing trade. Whereas Simon and Andrew leave behind a business and a livelihood, James and John leave behind *people*—a father and his hired hands. Such a departure leaves not only James and John vulnerable but also their father himself, who suffers a significant loss of strength and labor, perhaps himself no longer able to carry on all of the strenuous work of the fishing industry, and who might rightly be expected to disapprove of his sons' actions.

The stakes of the boys' participation in Jesus' ministry, therefore, are high. And yet because they are ushered into Jesus' inner circle and ultimately supported not only with Jesus' approval but that of their mother as well, their eagerness and enthusiasm are rewarded. When read from the perspective of their possible youth, the sons of Zebedee teach us to pay close attention to the actions and commitments of children. At the risk of anachronism, teenagers across the ages have embodied and continue to embody the best of human passion and commitment to ideals and a better world, even when both may seem impossible.

Even more remarkably, such youth have often succeeded in bringing adults along and helping us to reframe what we see as possible, practical, or even best. We can see such modeling in the relationship James and John have with their mother, the relationship Noah and Natalie have with their congregation, and more broadly, local and global responses to children who advocate for social and ecological change. The changes may not happen all at once, but young people have the potential to raise a community's awareness about injustice and urge us beyond complacency.

In the same community where Natalie and Noah lived, a group of high school students captured local attention when they too used their voices for change. Following the police murder of George Floyd in 2020, the high school's Black student association, Leaders of Tomorrow, participated in a community-wide Black Lives Matter rally. The president of Leaders of Tomorrow was met with hushed appreciation as she shared her experiences of racial bullying, profiling, and discrimination in the school. This young woman and the other students with her opened the eyes of both the school superintendent and the community, proving themselves to be leaders of today, not just tomorrow. In reflections after the event, the superintendent stated that he hadn't previously been aware of everything these students shared but personally promised that he would work to make things different. In response to the students' call for change, the school corporation has begun an honest examination of its policies; has added an anti-racism policy to the student handbook; has hired a diversity and equity officer; has instituted anti-racism training; and, under the direction of the new diversity and equity officer, has begun to rework disciplinary, high-ability, and hiring policies with equity in mind. When asked about his decision to make these changes, the superintendent replied simply that the voices of students matter.

Fishing for People

Churches would do well to listen more closely to the voices of children and students in our midst and to celebrate them for the gift that they are. When we read the call stories of James and John with their possible identity as youth in mind, the expansiveness of Jesus' call begins to take shape. We know that the ministry God is inviting us to participate in is not only for adults, for Jesus tells us clearly that God's realm belongs to the children (Luke 18:16). But James and John remind us not only that children hold a claim to the realm of God but that they are active coworkers in it. Some children are even called to lead adults in the work to which God calls us. This is the legacy of children like Noah and Natalie, the Islamic youth who spoke up for his community, the Leaders of Tomorrow president, and her organization.

When we read beyond the adult male-centric lens that dominated both the writing of and much of the commentary on the Scripture texts, we begin to see that Jesus' followers did not comprise an elite men's club. While some had wealth, others, like the struggling fishers in this text, likely didn't always know from where their next meal would come. Some may have been male, but others, like the women who discovered Jesus' empty tomb, were female. And while some were adults, others, like James and John, may have been adolescents, stepping out for the first time to discern God's call for their life without the safety and security of family that they had always known.

This kind of discernment is natural to the stage of late childhood and early adolescence. As children begin to understand themselves as members of a broader community and world, they want to find their place in it. Unfortunately, not every church encourages children to explore their place in these larger communities as a part of their faith. Rather, many fifth- and sixth-grade Sunday school classes emphasize learning doctrine, reciting creeds, or accepting Jesus. While these are all important and have their place, the power of each such affirmation is for the children who profess faith to live in such a way that their lives reflect the beliefs and the Savior they affirm.

As children begin to reach the stage of development that pays increased attention to the outside world, one discipleship tactic is to rein them in—to remind them of all the ways that the world outside of safe, close-knit communities of faith could potentially harm them. (I wonder if Zebedee had similar fears when he considered his children leaving the family fishing cooperative in which he could more closely observe their interactions.) This is an understandable impulse, especially as we take stock of the dangers associated with childhood, both in the first-century world and today. And yet today's church reaps the benefits from Zebedee's not choosing (or at least failing to succeed in) this tactic. James and John helped Jesus to feed the hungry, heal the sick, and preach the gospel in ways that set the stage for both the early church and our own.

An alternate approach to discipleship—the approach Jesus seems to have taken—is to listen closely to the concerns that capture the hearts and minds of the children and youth in our communities—to not only call children to follow Jesus, but to answer when they call us to do the same.

We live in a world where it is countercultural to take the voices of children seriously. As of this writing, the United States remains the only UN member nation not to have signed the UN Convention on the Rights of the Child. Whether in response to the COVID-19 pandemic, gun laws, educational funding, or any number of other societal issues, the needs and concerns of adults are continually prioritized over against those of children. Yet teen climate activists have taken the world stage clamoring for better environmental regulations, begging for today's leaders to take seriously the health and well-being of those who must live tomorrow. Yet in the United States and abroad, children and youth are excluded from voting on these very issues. Politics continue to curry to the interests of adults—especially wealthy and well-connected adults.

Within the church, however, we possess a unique opportunity to break down these barriers. Whether through baptism or affirmation of faith, many churches include children in the larger church body around the stage of adolescence, at least symbolically. In some churches this means that youth begin to stay in worship to listen to the "adult" sermon, or even take notes on it. In others, it means that service and offerings from youth are encouraged. Often such transitions lead to an encouragement that youth listen even more closely to adults. But in some denominations or church bodies, youth are even given the privilege to vote in congregational meetings, serve in regional ministries, and participate in "adult" committees as they enter into adolescence. When taken seriously, such privileges signal a countercultural interest and intentionality around listening to what the youth in our churches have to say.

When we listen in this way, the ministries that children lead us in can take many different forms as they point to the gospel. Noah and Natalie's Sunday school class empowered them and their classmates to speak a countercultural message to which at least some adults in their community heard and responded. The Leaders of Tomorrow club inspired their school corporation toward real change. But change doesn't have to be huge. In the same community, youth at Messiah Church, wrestling with growing too old for some of their favorite Halloween traditions, led their families and friends in dressing up and collecting for their congregation's food pantry during trick or treat. Together they now collect wagons full of food to feed the hungry each Halloween. When I was a sixth-grader, I remember showing up for a confirmation class one week to find an injured bird on the walkway. With the other youth in my class, we protested until the minister (who happened to be my father) relented and allowed us to pause our lesson and call animal control to help the bird.

Whether in large or small matters, the voices of children have the power and potential to make real change. In many cases when we listen, it is these very voices that redirect decision makers to the missional power of Christ's church—reminding us of the purpose and gifts that we share together as the body of Christ.

Whether we heed their voices or not, our youth are listening and watching. Just as surely as did James and John, today's young people sit in the boats with their parents, mending their nets. And just as surely they hear Jesus' call: "Follow me!" They hear his inclusion of all people, and of their own free will—often against the warnings of the adults who would shelter them—they respond. The role of Zebedee, and indeed his wife, thus shifts from sheltering and controlling those under their care to coming alongside of them, to keeping up the boat in their absence, to following them where they need to go, to supporting them, to amplifying their voices, and to trusting the good news that our Savior has come not only for the sake of, but to call into his mission, all people.

For Further Reading

Crowder, Stephanie Buckhanon. "Zebedee's Wife: A Shameless Mother (Matthew 20:20–28)." In *When Momma Speaks: The Bible and Motherhood from a Womanist Perspective*. Louisville, KY: Westminster John Knox, 2016.

Culpepper, R. Alan. *John, the Son of Zebedee: The Life of a Legend.* Minneapolis: Fortress, 2000.

Destro, Adriana, and Mauro Pesce. "Fathers and Householders in the Jesus Movement: The Perspective of the Gospel of Luke." *Biblical Interpretation* 11, no. 2 (January 2003): 211–238.

Hanson, K. C. "The Galilean Fishing Economy and the Jesus Tradition." *Biblical Theology Bulletin* 27 (1997): 99–111.

Murphy, A. James. *Kids and Kingdom: The Precarious Presence of Children in the Synoptic Gospels.* Eugene, OR: Wipf and Stock, 2015.

Questions for Discussion

1. Tell the story of a young person you know (either personally or through media coverage) who has taken a risk to stand up for something important to them.
2. In what ways do you think that the gospel Jesus preached may have been attractive to young people? In what ways may it have been particularly challenging to them?
3. What challenges do young people today face when they consider standing up for something they believe in?
4. How can adults support young people, especially those in our faith communities and larger communities, to stand up for their beliefs?
5. How can listening to the voices of young people help adults in our churches and local communities to live into our faith more deeply?

Chapter Four

The Gift of Listening

Mary at the Feet of Jesus

"Mary . . . sat at the Lord's feet and listened to what he was saying."

—Luke 10:39

The first church library I ever stepped into was in the basement of the church, tucked away in a dim room beneath the church offices. The effort to collect and save Bible commentaries, church histories, and works of theology was commendable, but regrettably, not many people passed by it. The result was more books acquiring dust and a hint of mildew than receiving regular attention. In contrast, the church library at St. Andrew Church is in the central quad that houses both the congregation's faith formation wing and their multiuse fellowship hall. The space is brightly lit, the bookshelves sturdy and dusted, and the collection is regularly tended. One cannot help but notice it.

While waiting for Sunday school to begin, children browse the rows of bookshelves lining the walls in between their classrooms, which are overflowing with board books, children's Bibles, and other illustrated gems. It has even become a church practice that in lieu of trinket gifts for the Sunday school teachers, children and their families annually dedicate new books to the church library in their teachers' names. But most importantly, this is a space that is not unduly monitored or policed. Children of the congregation and guests alike not only are allowed but are encouraged to pull out, read, and take home books from the attractive, low-sitting shelves. Often a Sunday school teacher or other friendly adult or older child can be found pulling out a book for a younger child, recommending it as a title they particularly enjoy.

The church library at Brown Community Church is set up differently. Since this congregation is a mission development worshiping in a school gym, the books are not set permanently on sturdy wooden shelves but are wheeled out into the welcoming space every week on metal library carts. Nevertheless, the care with which the books are collected, cared for, and distributed is strikingly similar. Most notably, due to the limited amount of space on the rolling carts, the congregation's volunteer librarian, Bev, works carefully to curate a selection that addresses topics of faith and community spanning ages from the youngest infants to the oldest adults.

One of my favorite parts of this congregation's online worship during the COVID-19 pandemic was the weekly video "book moment" features arranged by the church librarian in which members of the congregation, from the youngest to the oldest, shared about a book they had borrowed from the church library through a door-to-door "book drop" program. Such sharing not only provided a way for us to be community together while we were apart, but it also strengthened the ability of each member of our shared body to uplift and encourage one another.

I remember Henry, at not much more than three years old, sitting on his mother's lap in their family living room and holding up a large, illustrated children's book for everyone to see. The book, *Bold Women in Black History* from the Little Leaders series, was a collection of biographies. Henry was squirming and didn't sit still the whole time he was talking, but he managed to share that his favorite story was the one about Harriet Tubman. His mom showed us the accompanying picture, and Bev asked why this story was Henry's favorite. "The stars," Henry said, referencing the shining constellations in Tubman's portrait, representative of the importance of constellations—and in particular the North Star—to the Underground Railroad. Bev thanked Henry, but before he was done, Henry smiled widely and told everyone they should read the book because they could learn about a lot of really brave and smart people. When Henry had completed his review, at least three people—two of whom I knew to be adults without any children in their households—had put a message into the online chat requesting to borrow the book when Henry was finished with it.

Sharing books and stories, whether through a recommendation, a book challenge, or a well-stocked church library, is a powerful means of building up community in the body of Christ. I think this is especially true because story time is an opportunity to learn about and from those in the room together, as well as to learn about ideas and cultures that go far beyond those gathered. Those stories shared become the basis for further learning on everyone's part; most importantly, they strengthen and grow our relationships with one another within and beyond the church walls.

Yet too often we don't take the time to listen to one another's stories, perhaps especially when they're coming from children or others whom we deem too "different" from us. This behavior is usually motivated by a closed-minded assumption that we already know everything we need to know about a topic—whether it's a list of the latest books to read or anything else—and it is particularly common with adults.

The danger in this attitude is illustrated by one of my children's favorite storybooks from when they were Henry's age: *The Interrupting Chicken* by David Ezra Stein. Stein's story of a father chicken reading his baby chick a bedtime story beautifully captures the experience of story time, at least from my adult perspective. The title illustration portrays a serious father and his bouncy baby chicken sitting behind an open storybook, reminiscent of Henry and his mother in that online worship service. There are word bubbles above each character:

> "This book is called *Interrupting Chicken*, right, Papa?"
> "Yes. Now, please don't interrupt the story!"

The story continues from there, with Papa attempting to read the little chicken bedtime stories but to no avail. When Hansel and Gretel are about to meet the witch, the chicken warns them. When the wolf happens upon Little Red Riding Hood's path, the chicken interrupts, "Out jumped a little red chicken, and she said, 'DON'T TALK TO STRANGERS!' So Little Red Riding hood didn't. THE END!" And the interruptions continue until the stories run out.

Papa Chicken grows increasingly frustrated by these interruptions. I suspect that even some of the most patient parents can, at times, relate to that. I'll confess that in my parenting journey there have been times when I've been able to relate a little too closely to the Papa who warns before even starting to read the story not to interrupt. I've been known to forestall questions with, "Shhh. Listen to the story and you'll find out!" Or, as the night wears on, "At this rate we'll never finish the chapter. If you say another word I'm going to stop reading for the night."

But in my better moments, I've discovered that answering these questions not only stocks inquisitive minds with ten more new things to ask, but it also opens rich and rewarding conversations. In fact, more often than not I've learned both from and about my children in the process. It's this realization that causes me to qualify Papa Chicken's perception of story time. While he may have thought his storytelling was repeatedly thwarted, in fact, Baby Chicken was not thwarting Papa's stories so much as telling new stories of her own. She was not afraid to claim her voice as her own and, eventually, by inviting her to tell her own story, Papa Chicken is smart enough to listen.

Now that Brown Community Church is meeting again in person, book moments are saved for special events rather than being a weekly feature. However, the carts of well-loved and well-tended books continue to sit front and center as the congregation enters to worship and study. Recently when my son selected a book from the cart, one of the pastors asked about his selection and said she would be interested to hear more about the story when he returned it. On our way home from church, William was already reading the book, matter-of-factly telling me that Pastor Von wanted to know more about it. Through these conversations, children like Henry and William are building a love of reading and developing a rich appreciation for the relationships and encouragement possible in a church community—encouragement that buoys not only children's faith but that of the whole community when we take the time to listen to their stories.

Much of why Henry's book talk stands out to me has to do neither with the content of the book nor with his review of it, but rather with the honesty and energy with which people received Henry's report. For the appreciation and response to his review in that small Christian community, Henry might as well have been a book review editor for the *New York Times.* His reception was not facetious but was rather a sincere desire to learn more about a book that Henry enjoyed and, perhaps, to connect with him in the process. It was, at its heart, about being community.

Human beings at any age are highly social, hungry for the gift of relationship that comes from sitting and learning together. The trouble is that as adults we often forget to make time for this remarkable gift, or like Stein's Papa Chicken, we lose our patience along the way. However, by reading with my children, I have discovered that sharing a story in community changes the pace and experience of it. The closeness of sharing a story together is rewarding, especially when it has been recommended by a librarian or friend, and the oral nature of reading aloud slows the story down. But the biggest gift is the interruptions.

Interrupting Martha's Story

Luke 10:38–42

The story of Mary and Martha in Luke 10:38–42 is often shared in community, and it is full of interruptions. At first glance, the story appears to be about Martha. Well, Luke's whole Gospel is about Jesus, but this story starts out about Jesus *and* Martha. If the story outside of Bethlehem was about the shepherds' visit to Jesus, and the story on the Sea of Galilee was about Jesus' call of the fishers, this at least feels like it should be described as Jesus' encounter with Martha. Martha, as the subject of the main verb "to welcome" (10:38), is the one who welcomes Jesus when he arrives at her village. The village is unnamed, and yet Martha—a woman—is named as the owner of the home where Jesus stays. That's no small accolade.

In one sense, we could say that Jesus interrupted Martha and Mary's routine when he came into their home. However, already in verse 38, Martha has received the peace of Jesus. The story doesn't say this directly, but it's made clear by her role as one who welcomes Jesus and his disciples. Jesus describes such hosts as sharing in God's peace, instructing his apostles, "Your peace will rest on that person" (10:6). Martha's story occurs as Jesus and his disciples are beginning their journey from Galilee to Jerusalem, proclaiming the good news of the inbreaking realm of God as Jesus sets his mind on what must come next. And Jesus prepares for this journey by sending missionaries on ahead of him with instructions about what to do and who to stay with. Jesus' own travels mirror these instructions, which make plain Martha's favored status as one who welcomes messengers of God's realm:

> Go on your way. See, I am sending you out like lambs into the midst of wolves. Carry no purse, no bag, no sandals; and greet no one on the road. Whatever house you enter, first say, "Peace to this house!" And if anyone is there who shares in peace, your peace will rest on that person; but if not, it will return to you. Remain in the same house, eating and drinking whatever they provide, for the laborer deserves to be paid. Do not move about from house to house. Whenever you enter a town and its people welcome you, eat what is set before you; cure the sick who are there, and say to them, "The kingdom of God has come near to you." (10:3–9; see also 9:3–6)

So it is that Jesus finds himself staying in Martha's home, accepting her hospitality, interrupting her ordinary routine, and proclaiming the good news from her courtyard.

The disciples who follow Jesus along his journey serve an important function, learning and teaching alongside him—and even, as we've seen, going ahead of him to proclaim God's realm. However, through glimpses into Jesus' proclamations and into homes and villages like Martha's, Luke also shows us the importance of the many other followers of Jesus who stayed at home and welcomed Jesus and his traveling disciples into their homes. These too were a part of the larger community that supported Jesus. They engaged in discipleship and service, though of a different kind, through providing a much-needed supportive role that was perhaps more akin to that of a church librarian than of the lead preacher. Each played a part in making sure that God's message was heard. Just as whole traditions would be lost without communities to tell and share them, Jesus and his disciples' traveling ministry would never have survived without welcoming hosts like Martha. And so, the Scripture affirms, the peace of the Lord rests upon her. There is much in this story that acclaims Martha's role.

However, like an impatient child (or Baby Chicken), already by the second verse of the narrative Martha's sister, Mary, interrupts her story. Instead of dutifully following along with the plot of arrival, welcome, and hospitality, as Martha expects her to do (Luke 10:40), Mary sits at Jesus' feet as though it's story time (10:39). I can't help but picture the many story hours I've attended with my children, both in public libraries and Sunday schools, as I imagine Mary cross-legged in a room of people crowding around Jesus, the master storyteller, to hear what he has to say. As Jesus weaves his proclamations of God's inbreaking realm for the gathered crowds, I picture the rapt attention of Mary and everyone around her—a story hour of the highest sort. Nevertheless, Martha, burdened with all of the work of hospitality for their honored guest, does not have patience for Mary's curiosity or interruptions.

For all of the magic that the children's librarian assigned to storytelling is able to weave, an observant parent will notice another children's librarian moving effortlessly in the background, making sure the doors are unlocked; propping up books and puppets for her colleague to use; passing out egg shakers as children chant and sing along with the story; and guiding parents and children to bathrooms, tissues, and other necessities along the way. The tasks of this busy, organized librarian are easier to overlook than the storytelling magic of her partner, but they are just as important in order for the event to run as smoothly as it does—or even to happen at all.

So as I read about Martha tending to all of the practical needs that make Jesus' proclamation possible, I picture her scurrying around like that second children's librarian, trying to keep track of all the details for her guests. Of course, Martha is not a librarian, nor is Mary simply one of Martha's other guests who came to their home to hear a great storyteller. They are sisters who not only live together but who are responsible for one another. Although we can't know for sure, the absence of any male figure in the story (other than Jesus) strongly suggests that Martha may have been Mary's guardian. For those familiar with the names Mary and Martha, this might come as a bit of a surprise as you wonder, what about Lazarus? The Martha and Mary described in Luke's story are often associated with the women by the same name who appear twice in John's Gospel account together with their brother, Lazarus (John 11:1; 12:1), but this association is less than certain. The story of Jesus teaching in Martha's house is the only time that Martha and Mary are named by Luke and is likely the only time these particular sisters are mentioned throughout the New Testament. Martha and Mary were common names among first-century Jews, with multiple Marys named in the New Testament alone. In order to understand the sisters' story in Luke's account, it's therefore helpful not to confuse them with the Martha and Mary whom John describes.

John locates his Martha and Mary in the village of Bethany (John 11:1), just outside of Jerusalem. Jesus also visits this village in Luke's Gospel, but only *after* he reaches Jerusalem, a journey he's still undertaking when he meets the sisters in Luke's story. For Luke, Martha's village, which is unnamed, is one among many in the middle of a series of villages Jesus visits on his way to Jerusalem (see Luke 9:51; 13:22), rather than his last stop just outside the Holy City. Moreover, while John assumes an ongoing, affectionate relationship between Jesus and this family, Luke does not. Lazarus is described to Jesus by his sisters as "he whom you love" in John 11:3, and, notably, the sisters seem to have a way to contact Jesus personally in the first place. John also provides a narrative cue when he introduces Mary as "the one who anointed the Lord with perfume and wiped his feet with her hair" (John 11:1). In contrast, Martha's relationship with Jesus in Luke does not seem to be any closer than that of the others who host him along their way, and nothing further is said after this encounter about an ongoing connection between Mary and Jesus. Luke certainly does not provide a narrative cue to remind us about this encounter, nor does John indicate any knowledge of when Martha and Mary hosted Jesus and his disciples. Thus, while we can't be certain whether the same Mary and Martha are intended in each Gospel, it seems unlikely. Moreover, since Martha had a living brother in her household, his position within their family would have made Martha's ownership of a house less likely.

That brings us back to Martha's story. Ultimately, whether or not Martha has a brother Lazarus who owns a different home, Luke tells us that Martha "received [Jesus] into *her* house" (Luke 10:38, emphasis added). This is a gesture of first-century hospitality parallel to that which Jesus instructs his disciples to seek out. By receiving Jesus, Martha agrees to serve as his host, providing a place for him to eat and sleep—a home base from which he may engage in his teaching and healing (10:39). Martha sets the scene for Jesus's "story hour" to be a success. Moreover, while the many tasks with which Martha is occupied likely include the woman's work of hosting typical of the context (see, for example, John 12:1–8), Luke leaves us to assume that Martha's tasks also include those of the householder, more typically but not exclusively reserved for men. In other words, in working to make Jesus welcome in her home, Martha as a single woman is doing the work that would have been divided between two or more people in other homes.

Although Martha is understandably hurried, her role is not only one of busyness. As the householder, she takes a position of prominence and power from the moment her name is mentioned. She is described both as a woman and as a homeowner (Luke 10:28), a somewhat unusual pairing for her first-century context. The singular possessive pronoun "her" suggests that Martha is not merely a member of the household but the head of it. This is affirmed by her act of hospitality in welcoming Jesus into her home not just by preparing his meals but by providing his shelter—a role reserved for the head of a household—and, again, by her boldness to speak directly to Jesus on relatively equal grounds, as his host (10:40).

Although the head of a household in the first-century Mediterranean world was typically the oldest adult male in a family, in some cases there was no living man to fill this role. This could be due to the death of a father, a husband, or both, and in these cases, women were accepted and regarded as heads of household. This suggests a couple of things—first, that Martha is the older sister of the pair, with a role of authority over and responsibility to care for Mary, as demonstrated by the clear indication that the house belongs to Martha and not Mary (10:38) and Martha's later request for Mary to perform her share of the duties within the household (10:40).

Second, Mary's presence suggests that Martha has inherited their *father's* household. In their cultural context, women were transferred, much like property, from the households of their fathers to the households of their husbands. If the sisters had been married, whether their husbands were living or not, they would have moved separately to their husbands' homes. That they are still living together suggests that they are living in their childhood home, having been under the control and power of their father when he passed away. If their father only had female heirs, as we will here assume for the reasons stated already, then control of the household would have passed solely to the oldest daughter. The youngest daughter would likely have inherited some property rights—at least a dowry for when she married—but while living within the household of her birth, she would have come under the authority of her older sister, just as would have occurred between boys. Therefore, Martha and Mary are not cohosts, as they are sometimes portrayed. Martha is the clear leader of the family and so bears the responsibility of hosting Jesus and his traveling disciples.

In all of this, Martha seems both gracious and confident—open and willing to play the host. It is important to note that she welcomes Jesus freely and does not complain about the work involved; she complains only about her sister's lack of participation in this work (10:40). The issue for Martha, thus, seems not to be about Jesus' expectations of her, which she has taken on of her own accord, but rather the need for her sister to share more of the responsibilities of the household.

Rather than helping to provide for Martha's guests, however, Mary has taken up a place at Jesus' feet, listening to Jesus' teachings (10:39). Here again, the decision seems to have been voluntary. Jesus makes clear that Mary's place at his feet is by her own choice (10:42). Martha works to provide for her guests in order to ensure that they are able to rest and teach comfortably. In contrast, Mary chooses to learn from these guests, setting aside her household chores.

When confronted by Martha about Mary's supposed breach of protocol, Jesus affirms Mary's choice, saying that it is a good one

(10:42). At the same time, it is worth noting that he does not criticize Martha's work outright. In fact, Jesus relies upon the welcome that Martha provides, and his previous instructions to his disciples make clear that he knows this. Jesus' comments may imply that the anxiety with which Martha goes about her tasks is not needful, but he never suggests that the tasks themselves are unnecessary or that Martha should stop. If no one provided the hospitality that Martha offers, Jesus' teaching would not be able to continue. Rather, Jesus attempts to calm Martha's worries while refusing to interfere with either sister's chosen activity—Martha's to serve and Mary's to learn. Both act upon their own choice, and both behave as disciples in their own rights.

Children in the Story

Mary, the Girl at Jesus' Feet

Both Martha and Mary have a choice in how to follow Jesus when he enters their village; however, their choices are not entirely the same. We've seen how Martha clearly fills the role of host in multiple ways, likely adding further anxiety to her service, since she must fill the traditional expectations both of a male head of household and his wife. She holds both authority and responsibility in her household and attempts to exercise this in appealing to Jesus. Mary, on the other hand, remains more of an enigma in Luke's text. We know her only in relation to others—first as a sister to Martha and then as one who sits at the feet of Jesus (Luke 10:39).

As a younger sister in Martha's home, Mary would have been compelled by her culture to show respect and obedience to Martha. In this sense, Martha is correct to expect Mary to help with household chores. However, the posture that Mary takes in the presence of Jesus places her in another role—that of a student. The Greek word *mathetes*, translated as "disciple," carries the meaning of learner. And, like Mary, students in both Roman and Jewish schools in the first century typically sat at the feet of masters in order to learn. Again, it may be helpful to picture a library story time.

Mary is not simply described as coming to hear Jesus preach, or as listening in on his message. Luke tells us that she was sitting at

Jesus' feet (Luke 10:39). The Lukan author only uses this image of sitting at a person's feet two other times. The first is to describe the posture that the Gerasene man from whom Jesus exorcised a legion of demons took when he wanted to become Jesus' disciple (8:35–39). The second time is in the Acts of the Apostles, which most scholars describe as a sequel of sorts to Luke's Gospel. In Acts, Paul describes his education this way: "I am a Jew, born in Tarsus in Cilicia, but brought up in this city at the feet of Gamaliel, educated strictly according to our ancestral law, being zealous for God, just as all of you are today" (Acts 22:3).

To sit at the feet of somebody means to learn from and attach oneself to that person as a disciple. Comparatively, as a doctoral student, I figuratively sat at the feet of my *doktorpater* (doctoral advisor), learning both the facts of biblical studies and how to embody that knowledge as a way of being and living in the field. In college, I remember sitting cross-legged on the floor of the student union during the community talent shows. Most captivating in those performances were the four- and six-year-old son and daughter of the campus pastor. In turn, each of them stood in the midst of our room full of college students, telling Bible stories from heart. I'm certain I've never listened to a Gospel story more closely than I did when, in turn, they relayed the story of Jesus' temptation—complete with gestures, articulation, and emotion. This, I later learned in seminary, is the way the first audiences of the Gospel stories probably heard them told. And it is a powerful pedagogy, indeed.

While Luke describes many people learning from Jesus, he does not use the concept of learning at the feet of the teacher lightly. Through the simple act of seating herself before Jesus to learn, Mary apprentices herself to him. She signals that she is interested in taking on a kind of discipleship that's different from the one her sister has filled. This may be why Martha does not appeal to Mary directly for help but rather implores Jesus to ask her (Luke 10:40). Martha recognizes the shift in power that has taken place through which Mary has removed herself from Martha's domain and placed herself under Jesus' authority instead. Like James and John who leave their father with the boat and hired men, Mary is leaving behind her responsibilities in Martha's household to sit at the feet of Jesus.

On the one hand, as we've already seen, Mary's actions involve choice. Jesus is clear on this. No one is made to follow Jesus by force. But on the other hand, Mary's choices are limited by her position within the social hierarchy of her household, whether that household is that of her sister Martha or the new household Jesus is building as a family of God. So what is "right" for Mary becomes a discussion between two householders rather than a discussion between either authority and Mary herself. Mary can choose whether to live under the authority of Martha or Jesus, but as an unmarried female with little or no property or wealth, Mary has little authority for herself. This would be true whether Mary was a child or an adult; however, when we read this text with eyes toward the children who may be hidden in plain sight, there are now several clues that Mary may not yet be an adult.

To begin with, Mary lives in Martha's household, under her authority. That Mary is under Martha's authority at all means that Mary has no living father, brothers, or husband in whose household to reside. As an orphan, Mary finds herself in Martha's care, most likely in the house of their birth after the passing of their father. Their father's passing may have made it more difficult to arrange marriages; however, the existence of a house and Martha's presumed ability to host suggest that the sisters are not destitute and so marriages would have been both possible and desirable, especially for Mary as the younger sister who did not inherit the household for herself. It can be expected then that once Mary reached marriageable age, somewhere in her mid-to-late teens, a spouse would have been found and she would no longer have resided in the house of her sister but of her husband. That this has not happened suggests that this Mary is, at least, a young maiden (like Jesus' mother when the angel first spoke with her), and possibly even a considerable bit younger.

Supporting this, Luke describes Martha as a woman (*gunē*), a word applied to females past marriage age, suggesting both social and physical maturity; however, Mary is only described relationally as Martha's sister, with no indication given of her maturity. And unlike the young interrupting Baby Chicken, Mary herself is never given a voice. Instead, she is portrayed consistently within a role of subservience—either under Martha's authority or that of Jesus. Such a position highlights the lack of self-determination granted to Mary within rigid first-century household structures, suggesting, though not demanding, a younger age.

Similarly, the ambiguity of Mary's age is portrayed in her role as a student. When Paul speaks of his studies under Gamaliel, he seems to be referring to his formative years; by contrast, most interpretations of Luke 8 assume that the Gerasene demoniac was an adult. Moreover, if Mary's position at Jesus' feet suggests that Mary is to be included among Jesus' growing group of disciples in Luke's Gospel, then we have already seen that this is a mixed-age group of learners. However, while not all students must be children, as demonstrated by the adults in Jesus' core group of disciples, childhood was and is the most common stage at which people devote themselves to learning.[1]

Learning and the desire to learn are common to human nature, but children have a particularly strong capacity for learning. With a driving need to discover "how" and "why," children are naturally drawn not just to the acquisition of knowledge but to relational and experiential learning that helps them to understand and interpret the world around them. Paulo Freire names this difference "cultural interpretation" over and against "narrative teaching" and maintains that such active involvement in the task of learning is necessary for liberation.[2] In oral cultures such as that of Mary, Martha, and Jesus, such dynamic learning occurs through an interchange of ideas involving both the teacher and the student. Scholar of orality Tex Sample explains, "Traditional/oral people do not learn by 'study,' but through apprenticeship."[3] Even in predominantly literate and postliterate cultures today, children learn what it means to be a Christian by how we speak and what we do at home and at church. In an oral culture, relationship and experience dictate meaning and are key, especially for children. This may have been even more true for Mary in seeking adult role models as an orphaned child. By seating herself at Jesus' feet, an action that Jesus himself names as a free and conscious choice (Luke 10:42), Mary chooses this learning relationship.

Other Children in Martha's Household

It is unlikely that Mary is the only child learning at Jesus' feet in Martha's house. Although it makes the most sense for Mary to have been living in her sister's household due to their father's death in Mary's childhood, it is at least theoretically possible to assume that Martha, as a grown woman, had already married and herself been widowed before their father's death. While deeply tragic, this would not have been uncommon in the first-century world due to frequent age differences between married couples and shortened life expectancies. If this were the case, in addition to Mary, Martha may have been responsible for small children of her own. Given the small living quarters in their village context, such children, like Mary, would have certainly been underfoot.

Even if Martha does not have any children besides Mary living in her household, children likely would have been among the villagers who come to Martha's house to greet Jesus. We know from various Gospel stories that it wasn't atypical for older children, just like adults, to seek Jesus out after completing their work or perhaps after leaving aside their work to find him. We have seen and will continue to see this in most of the child characters studied in this book—the shepherds, James and John, and the boy whose lunch Jesus uses to feed the multitude. Jesus' teachings were not reserved for adults—particularly in the household setting, where young children were most likely to be found. In addition, in many cases, adults seeking out Jesus may have brought young children with them in order to obtain Jesus' blessing for their children (as in Luke 18:15–17), or because the children themselves were interested or curious. They may also have done so simply out of necessity, especially with nursing infants and toddlers.

For this reason, scholars of early Christianity are becoming increasingly aware that the household settings in which Jesus taught were likely filled with the sounds and voices of children. But children weren't simply a distraction from what Jesus taught—the adults in their lives were likely unfazed by their presence, as having children around was a fact of life—rather, they would also have listened to and learned from Jesus. Although we create child-centered learning environments in the twenty-first century such as library story times and Sunday school classes, it's not lost on me as a parent that children—even the youngest toddlers—have very sharp ears. While they'll often ignore our "boring adult talk," I've found that children have an uncanny ability for discerning when the conversation gets interesting and for picking up all kinds of details that I sometimes wish they had missed. While I may wonder if my children are "getting" anything from a sermon in church while they are fidgeting, coloring, and what not, I am continuously amazed by the gospel insights they later reflect on at home. I've experienced this to be especially true during online worship in which my children are allowed, like Henry, to wiggle and be comfortable in their own space and so be able to concentrate more on what they are hearing.

Similarly, first-century children were accustomed to hearing stories told in their households. A few stories may have been specifically tailored for them, and the others, while directed to adults, caught their attention and helped them to learn something about living and being in the world. In the intergenerational space of the household—particularly at leisure hours, over meals, or in the presence of a guest such as Jesus—children and adults learned together through the telling of stories and the sharing of hopes for God's inbreaking presence. In all of these activities, the boundaries between adult space and child space would have overlapped—even with regard to enslaved children present in the mix—allowing Jesus' teachings to have connected with children in their own ways and through their own understanding. Occasionally a little child may even have raised her voice to ask Jesus a question or to respond with a celebration or concern about a point he had shared, thereby creating a natural flow of intergenerational learning together.

Welcome Interruptions

If you ask children what the correct routine for bedtime is, chances are that the answers you receive will be as varied as the children you are asking. Many bedtime routines involve a story, but not all. And how many stories are read, who reads them, and how and where they are read will also vary. Even in the different libraries my family has frequented over the years, I've found that there are different routines and traditions for "story time." Not every librarian sings the "Quiet Song" about hands crawling into laps and bubbles settling in mouths. Some librarians read from large, oversize books, and others read from ordinary ones. Sometimes it isn't even the librarian who reads. But whoever reads and however they do so, library story time in all of my encounters continues to be a magical event.

In a way, the same can be said about discipleship. Sometimes we may get it into our minds that there is only one way of being a disciple. Most often when we're thinking about the New Testament text, that will involve laying down our nets like James and John, following Jesus across the countryside, and becoming fishers of people. But Martha and Mary remind us that there are lots of other ways to be a disciple of Jesus.

Even though Martha doesn't physically join Jesus on the road to Jerusalem, she follows in his example by offering hospitality to him and, in so doing, proclaiming the good news of God's realm within her village—as do all of the other hosts who welcome Jesus and his disciples in every village they visit. To use Jesus' words, God's peace is with them.

Mary demonstrates another aspect of discipleship. Although we don't know whether she followed Jesus away from her village or stayed with Martha when he left, Luke makes clear that Mary has committed herself to a lifestyle of discipleship. And when we expand our definition of discipleship to understand that Jesus' followers included all of those who supported his ministry, whether traveling or at home, then it doesn't really matter much that we don't know what Mary chose for her future. Instead, paying attention to Mary's embodiment of discipleship in the present can help us to reframe and develop the aspect of discipleship connected to learning, which Mary models.

Christian education ministries, including church libraries, Sunday schools, and even oral storytelling times, embody this aspect of discipleship the world over, teaching young children Bible stories just as surely as librarians instruct their students or parents read their children bedtime stories. In this way, students simultaneously absorb the stories of their faith and the care of the faithful leaders who teach them. Those same teachers are fed in the faith by the smiles and questions of their pupils, who effortlessly make the old stories new again and sometimes even imagine the possibilities if we were to change the ending. Or at least that's the ideal way it can work when we recognize the holy exchange that occurs and the relationships built in these classrooms.

The dynamic interchange that happens when one chooses to teach and another chooses to listen is a blessing on all accounts. Although Luke doesn't tell us Jesus' exact words while Mary is seated at his feet, we know that he was teaching about the realm of God and the work of God's presence on earth. The core of this message is encapsulated in his first sermon in Nazareth:

> The Spirit of the Lord is upon me, because he has anointed me to preach good news to the poor. He has sent me to proclaim release to the captives and recovery of sight to the blind, to set at liberty those who are oppressed, to proclaim the acceptable year of the Lord. (Luke 4:18–19)

In short, Jesus' teaching is about liberation. And seated at his feet, freed from the demands of her sister's home and called into the simultaneously rewarding and demanding service of God's realm, Mary is liberated.

The exchange between Jesus and Mary as teacher and student doesn't only interrupt the functioning of Martha's household (and very possibly Jesus' own message); it also interrupts Mary's vision for what her life may hold. This is why bell hooks, an expert on pedagogy, calls the classroom a "radical" place. And Richard Shaull, in his preface to Paulo Freire's *Pedagogy of the Oppressed*, concludes, "There's no such thing as neutral education. Education either functions as an instrument to bring about conformity or freedom."[4] In dialogue with Jesus, Mary learns what it means to be a disciple. For Mary, discipleship means learning from and with Jesus the teacher and following Jesus the liberator as together they make sense of the world in which they live.

Sometimes it's easy to bypass a child's question, to write it off as unimportant or even frustrating. It can be tempting for educators, even or especially Sunday school teachers, to fall into what Freire calls "narration sickness"—the simple imparting of facts and figures rather than encouraging discovery or understanding. Sometimes it's even tempting for the students. Martha came to Jesus looking for a simple decision—for a fact to be imparted—but he pushed her to think about what she was asking on a deeper level. Jesus frequently frustrates his disciples—and many of us—with parables that have similarly obscure meanings. But the point isn't to frustrate or even to hide; it's to encourage deeper thinking.

And this is where the persistent nature of many children comes in handy. I think again of the little chicken who has so much enthusiasm she simply cannot allow her father to finish a story with an unhappy ending when she knows how to fix the problem. She isn't willing to accept the way things have always been and is eager to change things for the better, even to the point of writing her own story. I also think of my own children and their constant "whys" and "hows" that have accompanied so many bedtime stories.

Children don't back down easily, and they rarely accept simple answers or platitudes when there's a deeper truth to be known. No matter how many times my children have been shushed, they keep asking questions about our stories, keep demanding to know more, and, in the process, keep pulling me along in their explorations. Mary herself, by not coming as soon as Martha made known her concerns, gives space for Jesus to teach both her and her sister about the deeper meanings of discipleship.

It strikes me that when Jesus answers Martha, not only does he refuse to interfere with Mary's learning, but he also actively expands each sister's opportunity to learn by not defining either's role. Instead he replies, "Martha, Martha, you are worried and distracted by many things; there is need of only one thing" (Luke 10:41–42). Although Jesus goes on to say that Mary has chosen the "better part," he doesn't directly name what that better part is. Jesus leaves it to the sisters and those gathered to wonder over what the "one thing" really is.

Commentators across the ages have joined in this wondering, although often the wondering is cut short by a desire to narrate and define. For this reason, some study Bibles tell us that the roles of listening and studying are more important than the roles of welcoming and cooking. These are attempts to box each sister into predefined behavior. But if we resist this temptation and, following the example of bell hooks, transgress these boundaries, Martha and Mary can lead us to many more possible understandings of active discipleship.

In the Christian education world, these kinds of pedagogies are best embodied in programs such as Catechesis of the Good Shepherd and Godly Play that encourage teachers and learners to wonder together, although there are components to this open-ended pedagogy in many other programs as well. The key in any program, however it's framed, is to be clear about the objective. Do we teach Bible stories so that children will "know" the classic stories or their simplified moral lessons—in other words, to narrate information? Or do we teach Bible stories so that through them children will be transformed by the inbreaking presence of God?

When put that way, most of us will opt for the latter. But the truth is, being open to transformation is hard work, and it often requires a change of mindset. Most basically, an openness to transformation on the part of a teacher requires a willingness to allow both the children and the story itself to interrupt their lesson plan. After all, Papa Chicken never would have gotten to hear Baby Chicken's very own story if he hadn't eventually allowed her to alter his bedtime plan. This all sounds good in theory, but if you were paying attention to my own bedtime story woes, it may not surprise you to learn that one of the hardest roles for me as a Sunday school teacher has been internalizing the method of "wonderment" that pedagogies like Catechesis of the Good Shepherd and Godly Play advocate.

Instead of narrating for children the meaning of every word and every symbol in a Bible story, these programs encourage the teacher to wonder aloud with a child, in much the same way that Bev did with little Henry. Rather than assume that the adult leader knows the answer, or that a single answer even exists, such wondering gives children the chance to explore the possibilities. Perhaps the signature example is the interpretation of Jesus' parable of the Good Shepherd. As children play with toy sheep and hear the words of Jesus assuring them that he is the Good Shepherd, that he knows his sheep, and that his sheep know him, the adult guide is instructed to ask the children, "I wonder what the names of these sheep are?" It would be easier, of course, to tell the children that they themselves are the sheep. I have seen that revelation take children weeks or months to reach, but the joy both for myself and the children when I am able to bite my tongue long enough to let them come to that on their own is immeasurable. Over the years, some children have surprised me by not naming themselves first when they come to this realization, but instead naming their neighbors, family, or friends—all people whom they recognize as important and valued in the circle of God's family.

Similarly, in play-oriented curriculums like Catechesis of the Good Shepherd or Godly Play, the free art that children create may not always be directly related to Jesus or a Bible story, but when it is, it comes from their heart. When I first began this sort of curriculum at Saint Andrew Church in Tennessee, some parents were skeptical at first. Then during Lent, Jenna, the five-year-old daughter of one of those parents, not only painted a beautiful picture of the cross to show her mother, but she explained in detail Jesus' love for us represented in the picture. While Bible story coloring pages have their place, such predetermined lessons don't leave space for the kinds of self-reflection that Jenna had engaged in. Jenna knew what she needed that morning, or perhaps what all of us needed, and she didn't allow anyone or anything to distract her from her confidence in God's love.

With Mary seated at his feet and demands for attention circling all around them, Jesus tells Martha, "Only one thing is needful. Mary has chosen the good portion, which shall not be taken away from her" (Luke 10:42). He invites those gathered to wonder and, in so doing, to discern for themselves what the "right thing" for them may be. In the swirl of questions and information that threaten to consume us, Mary's decision to sit silently at the feet of a teacher and master storyteller calls us into the quiet and attention of a master student. Together with Mary and Jenna and all of the students of God's realm who have and will come after her, we are called to interrupt the ordinary and to reimagine our world in light of the liberative gospel that Jesus has come to proclaim.

For Further Reading

Aasgaard, Reidar. *The Childhood of Jesus: Decoding the Apocryphal Infancy Gospel of Thomas*. Eugene, OR: Cascade, 2009.

Freire, Paulo. *Pedagogy of the Oppressed*. 4th ed. London: Bloomsbury Academic, 2018.

hooks, bell. *Teaching to Transgress: Education as the Practice of Freedom*. London: Routledge, 1994.

Hylen, Susan E. *Women in the New Testament World*. Oxford: Oxford Academic, 2018.

Lillig, Tina, ed. *Catechesis of the Good Shepherd: Essential Realities*. Scottsdale, AZ: Catechesis of the Good Shepherd Publishing, 2007.

Stein, David Ezra. *Interrupting Chicken*. 2nd ed. Somerville, MA: Candlewick Press, 2016.

Discussion Questions

1. As a child, what was your favorite storybook? What attracted you to it? Whom did you enjoy sharing it with?
2. As an adult, what is your favorite story (secular or sacred)? What attracts you to it? Whom do you enjoy sharing it with?
3. In what ways does imagining Mary as a child change how you hear the story of her sitting at Jesus' feet? In what ways might Mary's age have changed how she heard the stories and teachings of Jesus?
4. Thinking about the role of a disciple as a *student* of Jesus, in what ways are you practicing discipleship in your daily life? In what ways do you want to grow this aspect of discipleship in your faith journey?
5. Picture a child in your life (past or present). How can this child or others in your community help you as you grow in your journey as a disciple?

Chapter Five

The Gift of Sharing

The Child with the Fish and Loaves

> "There is a boy here who has five barley loaves and two fish. But what are they among so many people?"
>
> —John 6:9

During the COVID-19 pandemic, grocery stores across the nation found themselves unable to keep up with the demand for many household staples. As a result, pandemic quarantine became a time for many households in America to learn (or relearn) the art of baking bread. Being particularly wary of most things related to the kitchen, I was slow to catch on to this trend—so slow, in fact, that by the time I began considering baking bread for my household, all the yeast at our local grocery store was also sold out.

Around this same time, my spouse, as a pastor, was preparing to celebrate the first online service of Holy Communion with our worshiping community, Messiah Church, for which we would need bread. Drawing on a familiar recipe for unleavened Communion bread, which he often prepared with youth and First Communion students, our family set to the task of bread baking with no yeast required. Instead, our kitchen was filled with the aromatic scents of honey and molasses as my spouse taught our children to sift flour, measure ingredients, and knead dough. We watched with anticipation for those first loaves to emerge from the oven. Although it took a while to perfect the rounded shape that we were so used to seeing on the Communion table, we relished the soft, sweet product with excitement.

One of the greatest losses that I felt personally during the quarantine period of the COVID-19 pandemic was a separation from the eucharistic community. During much of the pandemic, both Messiah and my seminary community continued to celebrate the Lord's Supper online by gathering remotely, each with our own bread and wine set aside. The symbolic richness of kneeling alongside this communion of saints, eating from the same loaf, and drinking from the same cup was set aside in favor of health and safety.

At the same time, however, this shift in eucharistic practice introduced my family to a new and richly meaningful experience. After those first loaves of unleavened bread emerged from our family oven, marked in the center with a cross to indicate their liturgical purpose, our oldest daughter had an idea: she suggested that we deliver Communion loaves to her friends in the neighborhood who also worship at Messiah. Soon more bread was baked, more crosses marked, the small circle loaves were sealed into Ziploc baggies, and our daughters carefully loaded them into their bike baskets, "porch dropping" Communion bread across the neighborhood.

That Sunday when we saw friends and neighbors on our computer screen eating from the same loaves as us, albeit from a distance, I couldn't help but feel the blessing of the communion of saints gathered. The following week, before we could begin our own baking endeavor, one of those same neighbors called to offer a loaf of her own (leavened) bread to celebrate Communion. In the weeks that followed, our families baked in turn and our children biked around the neighborhood to deliver bread each Saturday. After bread returned more readily to the stores but our quarantine persisted, I sometimes hesitated, feeling too tired or overwhelmed to bake the special Communion bread. I suggested instead that we use crackers or a slice of packaged bread, but one of our children always clamored for that special, delicious bread. And so we continued to bake, we continued to share, our worship continued to be accented with the fresh smells of honey and molasses, and we were satisfied.

Feeding the Five Thousand

Matthew 14:13–21; Mark 6:30–44; Luke 9:10–17; John 6:1–14

The story of Jesus feeding the multitudes is a familiar one. It not only occurs in each of the four Gospels, but twice in Matthew and Mark—with Jesus feeding a group of 5,000 people in all the Gospels and another group of 4,000 in the latter two. Some scholars debate whether Jesus in fact fed two different crowds, or if the two stories emerged out of different oral traditions of one miraculous feeding. Either way, the plot remains the same, with one notable difference.

John is the only Gospel to mention a child. Jesus also features more centrally in John's account, leaving some commentators to speculate that this story fulfills the role of the institution of the eucharistic meal, which is absent from John's account of the Last Supper. The prominent participation of this child and John's connection of this story with the eucharistic meal is striking.

As in the other accounts of the miraculous feedings, John's story begins with a great crowd following Jesus to a deserted place, with Jesus and his disciples then discussing how they will feed so many people. While Jesus ultimately feeds everyone in each story, in John's account Jesus takes clear responsibility from the beginning. In the other Gospels Jesus tells his disciples, "You give them something to eat" (Matt. 14:4; Mark 6:37; Luke 9:12), but in John, Jesus takes this responsibility on himself, already having a plan in mind (John 6:6).

This small shift sets up a bigger difference between John's account of the feeding of the multitude and those recorded by the other Gospel authors. In some sense, Jesus is the host of each of these meals, but for John, Jesus' centrality is key. This is emphasized by John's description of Jesus "giving thanks" before distributing the loaves (John 6:11).

Just as praying before or after a meal is a common practice in many Christian households today, giving thanks for a meal was a common practice in first-century Jewish households. Typically the father, as the head of the household, would say words of thanksgiving over each meal. This is how Jesus begins his last supper with his disciples, and it is also how he begins the meal that he shares with this crowd of 5,000 people in John. Similar thanksgivings are also included in the accounts of the feeding of the 4,000 (Matt. 15:36; Mark 8:6).

What is significant in each case, though, isn't *that* Jesus gives thanks; it's that the Gospel authors chose to record his thanksgivings in each of these instances. Jesus eats many other meals in the Gospel accounts, and at most, if not all, of these meals we can assume a thanksgiving is said. However, the Gospel authors only seem to highlight this practice when it is significant to the message of the story. Moreover, while Jesus eats many meals in the Gospel accounts, he is rarely the host and so the one who would offer the thanksgiving. Jesus is more often the guest. Even the family table prayer I was taught as a child bids, "Come Lord Jesus, be our guest," as we give thanks for the food at our table. But at his last supper with his disciples and in the open air with the multitudes, Jesus is not a guest—he is the host. And as the host, Jesus is both the one to offer a thanksgiving prayer and to bid those who wish to follow him to be *his* guests.

But unlike a typical host, Jesus does not provide the food to feed the multitudes out of his own resources. This is perhaps where John's account of the story takes the biggest turn. In the other Gospel accounts, the disciples seem to look only within their own stores to feed the crowds, declaring that they only have five loaves and two fish—not nearly enough to feed a multitude (Matt. 14:17; Mark 6:41; Luke 9:16; see also a similar pattern with the feeding of the 4,000 in Matt. 15:34 and Mark 8:5–7). However, in John's account, the disciples either have no food of their own or are unwilling to share what they have with the crowds. Instead, Andrew reports to be aware of five loaves and two fish belonging to a child (*paidárion*) who is among them (John 6:9). Following this report, Jesus commands the disciples to make the people sit down. He then takes the loaves and fish, gives thanks, and distributes them to the people in abundance.

While John never goes so far as to suggest that in this story the eucharistic tradition is initiated, John seems to want to connect that tradition with Jesus' act of feeding here. Even the timing of the feeding is specified by John as around the Passover (John 6:4). And just as the other Gospel accounts describe Jesus himself distributing the last meal he shares with his disciples, so too in John's account of this feeding it is Jesus, rather than his disciples, who distributes the bread to the people gathered (John 6:11), emphasizing Jesus's role as host. As a result, for John, the Lord's Supper is shared not in an upper room but on the shore of the Sea of Galilee, and not among Jesus' closest companions but among a large crowd (6:2) numbering around 5,000 (6:10). And while often overlooked by those who make these eucharistic connections, it is perhaps most significant that this meal is prepared not by Jesus himself or even his appointed disciples (Matt. 26:19; Mark 14:16) but by a child (John 6:9).

Children in the Story

Children in the Multitude

When Matthew records Jesus' feeding miracles, he gives the count of those present as, respectively, four or five thousand men, "besides women and children" (Matt. 14:21; Matt. 15:38). This is a fairly typical way of counting in the first-century Roman world. In Luke's account of Augustus's census, it is Joseph, not Mary, who is required to travel to his ancestral town to be registered (Luke 2:1–4). Mary and their expected child accompany Joseph for this registration, but it is unclear how or to what extent they are to be counted (2:5).

More anecdotally, feminist readers of Scripture have long noted that women are often only mentioned in these and other ancient texts when acknowledging their names or presence is necessary to the narrative. So it is that Matthew 27:55 reveals that women had been following Jesus all the way from Galilee only when it is necessary to set up their presence as the witnesses to the resurrection. Childist readers have observed the same patterns with children.

This is an instance in which more-inclusive translations of Scripture hinder our ability to understand the full scope of the story. The NRSV translation of John 6:10 reads, "Jesus said, 'Make the people sit down.' Now there was a great deal of grass in the place; so they sat down, about five thousand in all." But the NKJV provides a more literal translation of the Greek: "Then Jesus said, 'Make the people sit down.' Now there was much grass in the place. So the men sat down, in number about five thousand." Here we see a distinction between the "people" (in Greek, *anthrōpous*), who make up the totality of the crowd, and the "men" (in Greek, *andres*) who sit down. The Greek word *anthrōpous* is in the masculine plural and can be used to refer to a group of men; however, it is also the term used most frequently to speak of obviously mixed-gender groups and humanity in a general sense. In contrast, the Greek word *aner* (pl. *andres*) is very specifically masculine and refers to *adult* men. When read together, it's possible that Jesus and the Johannine author simply chose different words to refer to the same people, but it's also possible and perhaps even probable that John here is choosing to differentiate from all the people to speak specifically about the men. This reflects the cultural practice of counting only men, which we see even more clearly in Matthew's account.

In other words, John's account assumes that the crowd consisted of more than just adult men. The presence of a specific child whose lunch can be offered makes this explicit. But before focusing on that child, it's worth noting that this was not the only child in the crowd. Both John and Matthew assume that there were many women and children present. That only makes Jesus' miraculous feeding *more* miraculous, since even more than 5,000 are fed. It is also why I prefer to talk about Jesus' feeding of the *multitude*, since we actually have no idea how many people were fed either in this story or in the story of the feeding of the 4,000. In this story, there could have been more than 15,000 people fed by Jesus since—among men, women, and children—men would have represented the smallest population group.

Building on this, it's worth noticing that the language Jesus uses to refer to those whom he is preparing to feed is the inclusive *anthrōpous*, appropriately translated "people" in both the NRSV and the NKJV (John 6:10). Jesus intends the food that he distributes to be for all people—regardless of age or gender. It's possible to get caught up in language here, since John says that Jesus distributed the food "to those who were seated" (6:11) and those John describes as sitting down are the men (6:10). One explanation could be that, as in more formal Roman meals of the period, the men were fed first, with the women and children receiving the leftovers. If this is the case, the women and children were included in the miracle, but not as equals. Such a reading requires careful attention to the cultural practices that Jesus and/or John may have been imitating and a critique of the value of such practices in the present day.

In practical terms, though, it seems unlikely that the women and children remained standing in the grassy area around seated men while they ate. Another explanation could be that John refers to the men sitting down only for counting purposes and does not pay particular attention to whether or not the women and children are sitting. In this instance, while the men may still have been fed first, it seems reasonable to assume that the women and children were fully included in the feeding. Such seems to have been Jesus' intention when he indicated the entirety of the crowd, asking Philip where they would buy bread for these people to eat (John 6:6).[1] This more inclusive reading echoes the inclusive overtones of God's creation of the world, in which humankind is made in God's image (Gen. 1:27; the Greek translation of Genesis that Jesus and John would have been familiar with uses the same inclusive term, *anthrōpous*). While it may not have been so in the other settings—especially the formal Roman meals that some think the Last Supper may have been modeled after—at Jesus' table everyone is fed and everyone is welcome.

Children among Jesus' Disciples

By recognizing the presence of children in the crowds whom Jesus fed, we can begin to see the importance of serving and welcoming children. By remembering that there were children among Jesus' disciples, we can begin to see that the children in this story were not only those who were served and welcomed but were also among those doing the serving and welcoming. In contemporary terms, there are many different ways that churches might include children in the Eucharist as more than just recipients. In some congregations, children serve by holding the eucharistic chalice, offering the cup of salvation to those who come forward. In other congregations, children may assist at the altar as acolytes, helping to set the eucharistic table, holding eucharistic vessels for the altar servers, or collecting used cups or wrappers. In still other contexts, children and families may bring the bread and cup forward during worship (often during an offertory) or work with the altar guild to prepare the meal before service. Or, as my own children did, children may serve by baking the bread that will be used for Communion itself.

In John's story of the feeding of the multitude, in addition to the child whose food was blessed, it is likely that children were among the disciples distributing food and collecting leftovers in the baskets. Like Luke, when John refers to disciples, he doesn't consistently intend only the Twelve. In this instance, when John describes the disciples serving, he could mean a smaller group (Philip and Andrew) or, more likely, the large group who followed and served him along the way. Practically, to feed and clean up after such a large group would require far more than twelve disciples to help Jesus with this task. So it's reasonable to assume that among the disciples serving in this way, there would have been women and children involved.

These disciples would have been together with Jesus when he sat down on the top of the mountain (John 6:3). Some of them may have been a part of the conversation with Philip about where to buy bread for the people to eat (6:5). Andrew's entrance into the conversation makes it clear that the conversation wasn't limited to Jesus and Philip alone. Children would almost certainly have been among the disciples sent out into the crowds to make the people sit down (6:10) and among the ones who presumably counted the people as well. Perhaps they would have assisted Jesus in distributing the bread, though to keep the eucharistic connections, John limits that role to Jesus himself. Certainly, children would have been among the disciples instructed by Jesus to "gather up the fragments" (6:12). In all of these ways, unnamed disciples, among them children, offered themselves in service in order to assist Jesus in feeding the crowds.

The Child with the Loaves and Fish

It's unclear which group the child Andrew mentions belongs to—the disciples or the crowds. All that we know of this child comes from one sentence: "There is a boy here who has five barley loaves and two fish" (John 6:9). This, though, is spoken by Andrew, who may be referring either to "here" as the location with Jesus at the top of the mountain—in which case the child would have been a part of the group of disciples—or to here in the larger sense, of the entire crowd.

Because these two possibilities suggest a very different participation in the events that follow, we'll consider each in turn. But first, some clarification is needed about a unique word used to identify this child.

The Greek *paidárion* in verse 9, typically translated as "boy" or "lad," is an unusual term. This is the only place in the New Testament where that specific word is used. Grammatically, the word is in the neuter gender, meaning it doesn't refer specifically to a boy or a girl. Although its root word (*paîs*) is a masculine term that is typically translated as "boy," in the Greco-Roman world, *paidárion* could refer to either a boy or a girl. Often this ambiguity is cleared up elsewhere in a text when names or pronouns are used. However, since the child is so quickly bypassed in John's narrative, there is not even an additional pronoun to help us. I prefer to translate this word as "child" rather than "boy" or "girl" to keep this ambiguity intact.

This specific term for "child" also presents some difficulty in determining the character's age. In the Greek world, many taxonomies existed that defined stages of childhood using different terms. Such taxonomies were common in the Greco-Roman world and offered as many disagreements as unities, making it impossible to determine an exact age from such an outside source. In one taxonomy, the Greek physician Galen applies this term to children between the ages of seven and fifteen.[2] But it's unlikely that the Johannine author would have been aware of Galen or any other physician's specific work let alone stuck strictly to these medical categories in his writing. On the other hand, the translation of "lad" or even "young boy" in several English versions assumes this child to be at the younger end of the childhood spectrum.

At best, these ancient taxonomies can give us a general idea of what's meant by *paidárion,* and that is a child who isn't yet an adult. Adding to that the only context clue we have from John's Gospel—that the child is described as traveling with food—it makes sense to assume that the child is not completely dependent upon traveling companions. Otherwise, it would have been the caregiver who had the food, not the child. This level of independence was typically ascribed to children in the first-century world beginning around the age of seven. While there is thus room within the age spectrum for the child to have been a bit younger or several years older, I tend to picture the child between the ages of seven and ten due to John's description of the child as child combined with the child's relative independence to be moving about alone and with a prepared meal.

The final hiccup with the word *paidárion* has to do with social status. There are several different words to describe childhood in the Greek language, and some of them have to do with family relationships; others simply describe age, and still others have to do with how a person relates to the rest of the community. For example, as we've already seen, the term we translate as "virgin" in Luke describes Mary the mother of Jesus as a young girl ready for marriage. In this case, *paidárion* indicates dependence. For that reason, it can be translated as either "child" or "slave" (sometimes rendered "servant" in contemporary English translations).

In the Greco-Roman world, much like in the antebellum United States, terms related to childhood were also applied to enslaved members of the household, whether child or adult, as a way of indicating social inferiority. It's therefore likely that this *paidárion* was enslaved and possible, even, that the *paidárion* indicated by Andrew isn't a child at all but an enslaved adult. Since approximately one-third of the population of the Mediterranean world was enslaved there is a high probability that both this *paidárion* and many others who followed Jesus may have, in fact, been enslaved. One of the dark sides of our Christian legacy is that Jesus never explicitly condemned the horrific abuse of one human being owning another. In fact, many of his parables assumed slavery as a matter of course, and as recent scholarship has made clear, such "allegorical or metaphorical slavery language depends on real slavery to make sense."[3]

Further evidence that the *paidárion* whose food is shared may have been an enslaved person can be found in that the specific kind of bread is barley loaves, typically regarded in this period as food for the poor, as well as the fact that the disciples are portrayed as taking this food without asking permission of any kind.

However, even if the *paidárion* in John's story was enslaved, that doesn't mean this person wasn't also a child. Children were frequently enslaved in the first-century world. Although the root word *paidárion* can imply an enslaved person of unknown age, the diminutive term that John uses here appears frequently in classical literature to refer specifically to children who were enslaved. So one very plausible reading of John's use of this unique word could be to indicate that the child referred to here is not only young but also enslaved. Given that this is the manner in which tradition history has also interpreted the *paidárion*, while the status of this person as free or enslaved remains unclear in John's narrative, I hereafter follow that tradition in assuming that, regardless of status, the *paidárion* is a child.

Such a child could realistically have been present among either the crowd who followed Jesus out into the deserted place or the more consistent group of followers—his disciples, broadly defined—who have been following him along his way. In either case, this possibility, and the flexibility of the word between the two groups—children and people of all ages who are enslaved—highlights the imposition that the disciples make by taking the child's food. Whether asked to share or not, this child had a status in the larger society that would have provided limited agency with which to decline the disciples' request. The level of this agency might be determined, in part, by where we locate this *paidárion* among those present with Jesus on the mountaintop. Was the *paidárion* part of the crowd or of Jesus's discipleship group?

Reading This Child as among the Crowds

One way of understanding Andrew's reference to the presence of a child "here" (John 6:9) in conversation with Jesus is that this child was among the large crowd who followed Jesus from the other side of the Sea of Galilee. This means that the child would likely have come from one of the Jewish fishing villages, such as Capernaum, along the shore. Since the crowd is near the sea (John 6:1), it's possible that this child works in the fishing industry, either within a household or as an enslaved laborer for a fishing cooperative—perhaps akin to one of the hired hands mentioned in the call narrative of James and John. In either case, after his resurrection Jesus calls out to his disciples who are on a fishing boat, referring to them as "children" (*paidia*) before feeding them loaves and fish on the lakeshore (John 21:4–14); the connections between this story and John 6 are easy to see. This postresurrection scene echoes the story of the child, perhaps a fisher, who provides loaves and fishes for the multitudes here.[4]

Whatever the work in which the child normally engaged, however, as a member of the crowd the child would have left that work for the day to follow Jesus. In this scenario, the child's motivations for following Jesus are most likely mirrored in those of the entire crowd: "They saw the signs he was doing for the sick" (John 6:2). Perhaps this child is traveling with family members.[5] Or perhaps the child has seen a friend or even a member of the child's own household benefit from Jesus' displays of power. Perhaps the child is encouraged that Jesus does not seem to show any favoritism based on class or age in working God's wonders. Perhaps the child is simply possessed by a sense of curiosity and wonder.

Whatever the case, this child chooses on this day to set aside whatever daily labor might await and to follow Jesus instead. Moreover, that the child has brought along food suggests that this choice is made with some forethought and planning. The child is not simply swept up in the crowd. This child *planned* to follow Jesus. The child prepared ahead of time for the likelihood that this detour might last into the day, and then set out to find Jesus. Despite the limited agency entailed in being a child and, perhaps, an enslaved child, this child makes a conscious decision to follow Jesus.

Reading This Child as among Jesus' Disciples

This choice carries over into the second possible explanation of the child's presence. Although it's often assumed that the child is a member of the crowd, at the point in which the child is mentioned in the narrative, Jesus is conferring privately with his disciples. It's in that semi-private context that Andrew replies, "There is a child here who has five barley loaves and two fish" (John 6:9). It is possible to assume that the generic reference to a child, rather than a named person, suggests that the child has arrived with the crowd. However, when one remembers that in John's Gospel account Jesus' disciples are not limited to the Twelve in his inner circle, it's also possible to imagine that the child is present not as a part of the crowd but as one of Jesus' large group of disciples beyond the Twelve (John 6:3), and that Andrew may not have been intimately familiar with all of them, especially if the child's enslaved status caused Andrew to unduly dismiss the child's identity. At the very least, it seems that the child is close enough to this inner group that Andrew has noticed both the child and the food the child carries. The term "here," then, may be used as more than just a generic indication of everyone present, but a way to associate the child with the disciples and so with the group gathered nearest to Jesus on top of the mountain.

If the child is among Jesus' discipleship group, two possibilities exist. The first is that the child is present as an enslaved person to one of Jesus' disciples. In this case, or if the child was brought along as the free child of one of Jesus' disicples, the child would not have been given an option in following Jesus and, as such, the child may or may not have identified personally as a disciple of Jesus.

A child following Jesus together with members of the child's household may have exercised less agency in this choice than a child who just came out to see Jesus for a day. If this child were an enslaved member of a household who chose to follow Jesus, the child would have had no agency at all. Household structures in the first-century Greco-Roman world demanded strict obedience of the head of the household, usually a father or grandfather. This means that if the householder decided to follow Jesus and demanded that his children, grandchildren, and slaves follow suit, they would have been expected to do so. We see this same sort of dynamic at work in the baptism of whole households in Acts (see Acts 16:15, 33; 18:8). In this case, the child may be among Jesus' disciples and even instructed in Jesus' teachings, but without full agency to choose to follow Jesus. Within such a scenario, the child, keeping pace with this group of itinerant missionaries, has resourcefully managed to gather food for another day of walking and listening, serving Jesus as he performs his signs. The disciples notice the food, though, and in that moment, regardless of whether the child desires to share, the choice may be taken away.

In contrast, the second possibility is that the child self-identifies as a disciple of Jesus, either independently choosing to follow Jesus or claiming discipleship after following as a part of a larger household. The New Testament, while regrettably condoning the practice, records cases where enslaved persons make the independent decision to follow Christ (Eph. 6:5–8; Col. 3:22; Titus 2:9; 1 Peter 2:18; and possibly Philemon). In this scenario, whether enslaved or free, the child's decision to follow Jesus has more consequences than a single day away from work. As we saw in the case of James and John, such a decision may have entailed the decision to leave behind one's entire household—family, belongings, and perhaps even the possibility of returning home (cf. Matt. 19:27). Especially for those with the most at stake due to limited agency and oppressive, patriarchal households, choosing to follow Jesus may represent participation in God's people in a manner akin to what New Testament scholar Shively Smith refers to in the context of later Christian households as "a sort of 'love offering' . . . [to those] who dare to consider that their life story transcends their immediate situation."[6]

Regardless of whether the child was among the crowd of Jesus' disciples, willingly or unwittingly, this child becomes a cohost with Jesus at John's eucharistic feast. As we have already seen, Jesus takes on the role of head of the household by blessing and distributing the meal; however, it is the child who serves as the provider (a role also associated with the head of the household and host) by supplying the initial food for the meal (as much as Andrew may discount its suitability at first). In contrast to Matthew's accounts of the feeding of the multitudes, in which women and children are mentioned only as recipients of the meal and only as an afterthought (Matt. 14:21; 15:38), John flips the script, placing this young, likely enslaved, child at the head of the crowd, serving alongside Jesus as a host to this remarkable meal.

Making Space for Authentic Embodied Service

The loaves and fish belonging to the unnamed child in John's account provide the basis for both the meal and the miracle. Without the child's preparations we cannot know for sure how or whether the crowd would have been fed. However, the Gospel provides very little information about the actual child. In fact, the child is mentioned only once—when Andrew initially signals the child out (John 6:9)—and after that all attention turns to the food the child has brought. Andrew asks, "But what are they among so many?" referring to the loaves and fish. Later Jesus takes the loaves and fish, gives thanks for them, and distributes them. The people eat bread and fish until they are satisfied, and the disciples gather up the fragments of food that are left over (6:11–13). Finally, the food is consumed and Jesus is praised, but the child is never mentioned again (6:12–14).

This silence about the child whose fish and loaves stand in for those of the disciples in the Synoptic Gospels persists in much contemporary commentary on this text. Perhaps in part due to a temptation to tell all six of the feeding stories in the Gospel accounts as a cohesive whole and in part due to the lack of information about the child, most commentators mention the actual child only in passing, if at all. And yet at this pivotal point in John's narrative, the child persists as a key hinge in the unfolding of the story, which serves not only as another sign of Jesus' identity, but to recount John's understanding of the institution of the Eucharist as a communal meal of thanksgiving, shared by Jesus in remembrance of the same. Uncovering this child's presence, then, veiled but not forgotten, can help us to understand and interpret this meal.

Although this child is sometimes praised as offering up a meal when nobody else would, a careful reading of John's narrative shows no sign that this is the case. Although it's possible to imagine a scenario in which the disciples polled the people about who had any food, or in which the child, noticing a problem, approached the disciples with an offer to share, John doesn't record any such events. Instead, immediately after being told that the child has the food (John 6:8), we find that Jesus has taken the food (6:11).

The agency of this (possibly enslaved) child thus seems to be bypassed in favor of the definitive action of Jesus, who (as has already been pointed out) acts for this meal in the powerful role of the householder. Among other things, such a householder typically provides and blesses the food. In one sense, the child therefore serves to supplement this role. However, if the child is one of Jesus' disciples, then as a member of Jesus' household, all that the child has belongs to Jesus. Jesus can therefore still be seen, albeit with the aid of the child, as himself providing the food for the meal.

In either case, the choice does not belong to the child. Praise for the child rightly rests in the child's preparation for the day, including arriving with food enough for one at least. However, John gives no indication that the child should be praised for the decision to share. Within the confines of the story, no such decision exists. As is the case with many children and all enslaved individuals, the resources that this child has so carefully prepared and guarded are taken for granted as public property and commandeered as such.

Enslavement in this time and place was in many ways quite different from slavery in the American antebellum South; however, in one most basic respect it was precisely the same—the stripping of individual agency and identity from individuals who, understood as the property of the free householder, did not have the freedom to make decisions for themselves. If the child is a disciple of Jesus, it would therefore be misleading to say that the child chooses to offer the meal to Jesus. If, on the other hand, the child is a member of the crowd, the possibility for choice more likely exists; however, even here, the power of adult and authoritative coercion remains high.

The choice to offer the food to Jesus isn't anywhere near as clear as it is often painted; however, as we've begun to see, this doesn't mean the child had no choice at all. The child chose to follow Jesus (whether for a day or for a longer term as a disciple). The child chose to prepare a meal. The child is therefore present and active among Jesus and those gathered in the deserted place that John describes. The child's resources are important to the well-being of the whole.

This mix of agency and predetermined decision makes up a lot of ministry with children. The power dynamics between parents and their children, adults and nonadults, simply don't allow us to pretend that children make every decision to serve completely uncoerced. Even as I think back to baking with my children, while I can celebrate that the decision to share with neighbors was their own, I would be lying if I didn't admit that as their parent I influenced them to help bake the bread to begin with. And they were also aware of the kind of sharing I as their parent would encourage as appropriate and kind. I don't share this to diminish my children's initiative in this good deed, but simply to recognize that when adults ask service of children there are power differentials involved.

Whether knowingly or not, churches today often parade children in a similar display of God's greatness in contrast to their meekness. The classic song "Jesus Loves the Little Children" says as much. Children barely old enough to earn an allowance are given offering envelopes and encouraged to tithe. Even illustrations in many children's Bibles depict children bringing small gifts, like flowers, to Jesus. I myself frequently give each of my children a dollar to put in the offering plate as a way of learning the embodied action of giving. However, when children aren't given a choice in their giving, these practices can become merely performative. In contrast, a local pastor is known for an annual stewardship message to children in which he gives each child four quarters along with a divided bank containing slots for giving, saving, and spending. He instructs the children to put one of the quarters in each of the slots but then leaves it up to them what to do with the fourth. This sort of message combines the best of embodied learning while also teaching children that they have the agency to make real choices about if and how they give.

Across various worship practices, children today offer their gifts in the tradition of John's *paidárion* by singing, dancing, acolyting, reading, reciting, or placing dollars in the offering plate. In each instance they are both really and truly contributing and, often, like John's *paidárion,* doing so with little or no true agency of their own. After all, is that dollar I give to my daughter to put into the offering plate ever really hers in the first place?

Recently I was in worship with my brother, his wife, and their daughter, Alaina, who had just turned two years old. I handed my children each a dollar to put in the offering plate and watched out of the corner of my eye as my brother handed Alaina a crisp one-dollar bill as well. The offering plate came to us first, and with minimal prompting to notice that the plate was in front of them, my children dropped their dollars into the plate. Moments later their heads shot around to look at their cousin who, having also dropped her dollar into the plate, was watching in horror as the usher carried the plate to another pew. "Oh no!" she cried. "He took my money!" The rest of the family did our best to muffle our giggles, as my brother and sister-in-law attempted to soothe Alaina. The dollar was never really hers, nor was the decision to give it. Yet she gave it—and once she did, Alaina deeply felt its loss.

On one extreme, it's possible that the child's participation in the feeding of the multitude was performative at best and coerced at worst—another way for the Gospel author to demonstrate how meager the material really was from which Jesus provided this abundant feast without any consideration of the child doing the giving. Likely having not yet eaten that afternoon, the child, like Alaina, may also at first have deeply felt the meal's loss.

Reading for the presence of children in the Gospels doesn't always mean that what we find will be idealistic, just as teaching children to embody worship practices isn't always idealistic. In fairness to my brother and little Alaina, I've had my own share of parenting moments in which, certain I was encouraging my children to do the right thing, I ended up realizing they weren't quite ready. My daughter Joanna's preschool Christmas pageant comes to mind. Frightened of performing in public, Joanna spent the entire performance crying and attempting to hide behind her costume. All the while, I smiled and snapped photos, glad to have her in the pageant without considering that she didn't want to participate. This was not my finest parenting moment. The challenge, as children like Alaina and Joanna have taught me, is to enable and encourage children to claim their own (albeit limited) agency to serve and to share their gifts in worship—and, for that matter, everywhere else.

It's happenstance, of course, that the probable age of this child in John's Gospel account, seven to fifteen, falls squarely within the range in which many contemporary churches admit children to the Communion table. Yet the term "admission" itself, which implies adult control and policing over the roles of such children, illustrates the tension in John's account. This child is at once both a host and a servant—free to prepare a foresighted meal and enslaved to the demands of those who, due to age and status, hold power over such a child as this. On the one hand, admission is precisely what this child experiences through acceptance by the adult disciples and teacher (Jesus), who elevate the child by making use of the child's food, and through the notoriety provided by the Gospel author, who chooses to tell the child's place in the story. By the Gospel's own accounting, it is only because of the child's resources—the food the child acquires, packs, and carries—that there is a meal for Jesus to bless at all. On the other hand, John's Gospel strips this child of a unique identity, if one was ever known by Andrew to begin with, and treats the child as a means to an immediate and a liturgical end.

I think again of my children baking and sharing our eucharistic bread. The simple truth is that I would not have thought to include our neighbors had it not been for the children's generous spirit—and, perhaps, their desire to see their friends. And yet their agency was tied up with my own. The children did not want to bake the bread at first; they would have rather been playing their video games. And then, when we decided upon sharing the extra bread with our neighbors, I volunteered our daughters to take the bread to the various houses without first checking with them about their willingness to play delivery girls.

Such sloppy respect for my children's agency is not new pandemic behavior. When I reflect upon the ways in which my three children have participated in worship in the past, I am aware that at the same time that my heart soars as I hear my eldest reading a Scripture passage in worship, I am almost always the one who signed her up. I have photographs of my shy middle daughter hiding behind other children, attempting not to be seen, singing at Christmas pageants I signed her up for without consulting whether she wanted anything to do with such a performance at all. And as I nudge my youngest up to participate in the children's sermon or calm his nerves when his father has borrowed one of his toys for a sermon prop without asking, I know that whether he enjoys the experience or not, the choice was never really his.

What happens, then, if we see this child host in John's Gospel not only as a model of generosity but also, and perhaps more importantly, as a reminder of the fragility of the freedom of the gospel (John 8:31–32)? What happens if we take seriously the truth that the child on the mountaintop was just as much a disciple as Simon and Andrew—with the same ability to contribute to (or withhold from) Jesus' mission as either one of them? What happens if we believe that the children in our congregations are just as much disciples—or for as far as that term will take them, church members—as any one of the "voting" adults? What happens if rather than pretending that children have something to offer we actually accept and acknowledge that they do?

Andrew points out the meager portions of the child's meal in order to demonstrate to Jesus the hopelessness of their situation. Jesus distributes that "meager" meal to a vast crowd, demonstrating instead not just what is possible with God but, indeed, what little ones such as this child are capable of as well. With Jesus and children serving together as hosts, the place of both in the realm of God is revealed.

There is much that remains unknown about this mysterious child with loaves and fish. Yet we do know that, according to John, this young person feeds a multitude. While granted little freedom of choice and gaining even less notice by the crowds whom he feeds, this child stands together with Jesus atop a mountain. Thanks to the foresight of this child, whose own identity will never be known, Jesus' identity was revealed in the breaking of the bread.

For Further Reading

Betsworth, Sharon. "John." In *Children in Early Christian Narratives.* London: Bloomsbury T&T Clark, 2015.

Glancy, Jennifer A. *Slavery in Early Christianity*. Oxford: Oxford University Press, 2002.

Martin, Joan M. *More Than Chains and Toil: A Christian Work Ethic of Enslaved Women.* Louisville, KY: Westminster John Knox, 2000.

O'Day, Gail. "John 6:1–15." *Interpretation* 57, no. 2 (2003).

Street, R. Alan. *Subversive Meals: An Analysis of the Lord's Supper under Roman Domination during the First Century*. Eugene, OR: Pickwick, 2013.

Questions for Discussion

1. When did you receive your First Communion? Or when were you baptized? Was participation in these rituals your choice, or did somebody make the choice for you?
2. At what age does your worship community admit children to the Communion table? Do children or youth help with the preparation or distribution of the Communion meal in your worship community? In what ways do children participate in these or other aspects of the worship service?
3. Recall a time in which a child or youth ministered to you in a meaningful way. What might you do in your own life or worship community in order to empower children and youth to participate more regularly in shared ministry?

4. Recall a gift that you have received from a child. Was it freely given? Why do you think the child gave this to you? How did you respond?
5. How can you nurture free will and agency among the children in your life and/or worship community while still guiding them in their discipleship journey?

Chapter Six

The Gift of Partnership

A Son and His Mother

"And Jesus gave him back to his mother."
—Luke 7:15b

Learning the Lord's Prayer is a rite of passage for many young Christians. In countless traditions, this prayer is recited weekly in worship. Often it is among the first prayers that parents and grandparents share at home with young children and also the last prayer uttered from the lips of many of the faithful departed. The combined depth of meaning and simplicity of language make the praying of the Lord's Prayer a spiritual practice common across the generations.

At First Church, both studying the meaning of and memorizing the Lord's Prayer is a part of the second- and third-grade Sunday school curriculum. Children in these grades meet with the pastor for a special evening series to study this prayer and the sacrament of Holy Communion. Because these classes take place during the season of Lent, a time in which the church also offers midweek evening worship, many of the children who attend this class join their families for worship afterward.

Eight-year-old Reagan attended First Church with her grandmother. When she entered second grade, she was excited to get to take part in these special evening classes. She arrived early to each class, since she rode with her grandma, who practiced with the choir at the same time. Reagan was eager to learn about the Lord's Prayer.

Practicing at home with her grandma, she was the first student to return to class with the prayer memorized—after attending only the first of four class sessions. As her pastor, I celebrated with Reagan and was grateful for her willingness to recite the prayer for her classmates as a motivation for them in their learning.

When we came to the Lord's Prayer in worship that night, my eyes were on Reagan, who was smiling proudly after setting down her worship booklet and beginning to say clearly and confidently from memory, "Our Father . . ." However, I was startled as Reagan continued, ". . . who art in heaven," while the rest of the assembly, reading along with the worship booklet, prayed, "Our Father *in* heaven." First Church typically prays the Lord's Prayer using the "traditional" language; however, during these evening services, we were using a worship booklet that printed the prayer with the "contemporary" wording. I hadn't prepared Reagan—or any of the other children—for this and realized immediately my mistake.

As those thoughts were running through my head, however, the prayer continued. And I realized I wasn't the only one who had noticed the discrepancy. Alene Bush, a quiet but confident matriarch of the congregation, had apparently noticed as well. As I stumbled, I heard Alene's voice ring out loud and clear from two rows behind young Reagan: ". . . hallowed be thy name." Without missing a beat, Alene had realized what was happening and joined her voice in synch with Reagan's. By the third line the other voices had faded out of my hearing, and I joined Reagan and Alene in praying the rest of the Lord's Prayer—in the traditional wording—from memory.

I noticed that others around us made this switch as well, as I suspect Reagan's grandma also did, the two of them sharing proud smiles when the prayer was finished and Reagan reached for her worship booklet once again. After worship, as I was putting out the candles, I overheard Alene, who had sought Reagan out, affirming her on how beautifully she had learned the Lord's Prayer.

I'm honestly not sure whether Reagan even realized that the words she had spoken were different from those spoken by the rest of the assembly in those beginning lines. But I do know that she noticed and responded to the affirmations of Alene and of her grandmother. And I know that, as Alene and others adapted to Reagan's confident prayer, we as an assembly were moved into action—into unity with one another. Perhaps not everyone who changed the words they were using even noticed, or understood why, but in that moment, I felt the fullness of what it means to be the body of Christ together.

The gift of such membership in Christ's shared body is in the recognition that in ways perhaps no one can anticipate, children and adults need one another's support and encouragement along the way. Reagan needed Alene and her grandmother's model and reassurance that she knew the "right" words. But both of these adults, who had raised their own children in First Church and had helped them learn the same words, also benefited from the gift of hearing these shared words of faith from the mouth of the next generation. At that time, Alene was joyfully preparing to welcome her first grandchild and, I suspect, could see visions of her interactions with her future grandchildren echoed in the warmth she shared with Reagan that evening. What's more, Reagan's confidence and excitement over her participation in worship fueled us all to appreciate God's presence and activity just a little bit more fully.

This interdependence—this need for and appreciation of one another—stands out especially in these milestone moments of faith formation because such milestones often reflect shared experiences. When I hear a child pray the Lord's Prayer for the first time, I always think of Alene, Reagan, and Reagan's grandmother. But I also think of the first time that I remember reciting this prayer with my own parents and of the moments of maternal pride when I taught the Lord's Prayer to my children. And I think of my father, who recited the Lord's Prayer with my grandmother at her bedside in the last days and hours of her life.

Whether it is the Lord's Prayer, a familiar hymn, a favorite Bible verse, or another shared tradition or text, it's important to remember that the sharing of the faith from one generation to another is not one-directional. Faith is a journey, and it is one that we take together. Young and old alike, we uplift one another on the journey. This sentiment is expressed beautifully in the title of a book that my own mother gifted her granddaughter shortly after her birth, *You Pray for Me, I'll Pray for You*, by Phil A. Smouse. With playful text accompanied by bright illustrations, this "read together" book invites young readers and their caregivers to pray together, alternating reading short lines of color-coded text with the goal of having fun talking to God together.

Such mutuality is the hallmark of relationships rooted in nurture and care. Parents, grandparents, godparents, and all those who accompany children along their faith journeys are able to do so because those children choose to continue forward with them. These journeys are taken together, each step of the way. Moreover, in the process, those who nurture others in their faith are taking steps in their own faith journeys as well.

We may not always contribute equally or learn the same things, but we learn together. We need each other. This is at the heart of what it means to be the body of Christ together. It's about shared relationships built and strengthened as we practice our faith together, just as Reagan and her grandmother practiced the Lord's Prayer.

That sounds easy enough, but the truth is that it's rarely so simple. Knowing that we need one another can put an engrained White Euro-American sense of self-sufficiency and independence to the test. Nevertheless, when we pause to adjust ourselves to one another, our voices can join in synch, and an old practice can become new again.

Comfort in Community

Luke 7:11–17

The first-century city of Nain is located in the southern part of the region of Galilee, an area well traveled by Jesus and his disciples, particularly at the start of his ministry. It was a predominantly Jewish town, built after the same manner of most cities in this time. The gates of the city served to protect its inhabitants from invaders as well as to mark out communal spaces. The dead were typically buried outside of the city, with both ritual and health practices in mind. It is therefore not unusual that Jesus and his companions would have encountered a funeral procession at the city gates.

Death was commonplace in the first-century Mediterranean world. A combination of diseases (typically carried through contaminated water and food), physically rigorous labor, and lack of consistent medical treatment meant that life expectancy in that time and place was, on average, significantly lower than it is in most places today. As we have already seen, infant and child mortality rates were particularly high. Thus, death and mourning in one's community and even family were simply a way of life for most people.

What makes the gathering of mourners in Luke 7 different, then, is not the simple fact of mourning, but rather the particularities of the deceased and the one who mourns for him. The person on the funeral bier is identified as a *neaniskos*, Greek for "young man." In the first-century world, this term was typically applied to boys between the onset of puberty and marriage, a phase that many today think of as youth or even an extended adolescence. Since boys typically married at a slightly older age than girls in this time period, the stage could have extended into the late teens or even twenties. In many cases, older youths might have begun to take on many of the cultural roles associated with manhood in their jobs, and even military service. However, as with girls, first-century Judean culture continued to view marriage and children as definitive marks of adulthood for boys, and a young man in this stage of life would have relied upon his family to help arrange his marriage, as well as to provide other continued social supports. The young man described in this Gospel story likely fell somewhere within this liminal stage, anywhere between ten and twenty years old.

Childhood illness and malnutrition in this time period meant that it was common for young children and infants to meet untimely deaths; however, the situation improved by the time of adolescence, with youth and young adult years described as one's prime, while early childhood and old age were riddled with the specter of death.[1] This means that while it was not uncommon for parents to bury their children, it was less common for them to bury a son at this stage of life—no longer young, but not quite grown. This is because such a young person had matured past the early dangers of infancy and the young childhood stage and was not yet susceptible to the vulnerabilities of old age.

Age is not the only exceptional quality of this funeral procession. Luke emphasizes that in this instance the family is not only burying a child but an *only* child. Mourning in Second Temple Judaism was typically a communal ritual, something in which both parents would have participated, together with members of their family. Especially since this youth had passed the age of young childhood, it would have been expected for his mother and father to mourn and bury their child together. Yet the mother alone is named. The child is described as "his mother's only son," with no reference to his father (7:12). Soon the reason for this unusual designation is made clear, when Luke explains that the woman is a widow. The loss of her son is not the first loss for this woman, therefore, since she has already lost her husband—his father.

All of these revelations may seem commonplace to readers familiar with the story. However, I lay them out in this way because that is the way Luke presents them. Luke begins with an ordinary funeral scene and then reveals each bit of surprising information as a series of revelations that lend greater gravity to the situation as each anomaly is uncovered. The word order is intentional and draws out, piece by piece, the magnitude of the tragedy. While at the beginning Luke's audience may have experienced grief at the mention of a funeral procession, by the end this is transformed as a more profound sense of loss is conveyed. The point is to recognize the tragedy.

Only after we fully appreciate the tragedy of the woman's situation does Luke clarify that this mother is not really alone because "with her was a large crowd from the town" (7:12). This crowd represents the support of the community, which is fulfilling the cultural obligations for mourners to cry out at the boy's death but also offering their embodied support for the family of the deceased—in this case a widowed mother.

In my experience, parenting in a White suburban context can too often become narrowly focused on the independence of an individual or a single family and their achievements. In contrast, womanist scholars recognize the contributions of "other mothers" in the raising of children—grandmothers, aunts, neighbors, and others who form the community that helps to care for a child. Such communal support is not limited to African American contexts, however. In a predominantly White Pennsylvania steel town, Reagan's faith was nurtured by her grandmother and by Alene Bush, who as a retired school teacher stood in as an "other mother" for countless children at First Church, encouraging and affirming them in the ways she knew she would want her own grandchildren to be encouraged and affirmed.

While Reagan experienced this through prayer, my own children have experienced this communal affirmation primarily through music. In fact, my oldest, Becca, first heard violin music played by none other than Alene Bush at First Church. Even as a toddler she was transfixed. At three years old, though, Becca's love for music grew when she saw then-ten-year-old Emma playing violin in worship at St. Andrew Church. By the following year, Becca was enrolled in violin lessons with Katherine Mansouri, who was also the children's choir director at St. Andrew, and Mrs. Mansouri invited Becca and Emma to play a simple duet on Christmas Eve. My children are not musical prodigies, and their musical performances in worship have not always been perfect, but over the years, invitations to play and affirmations of their musical talent at various stages of accomplishment have nourished them both in their musical pursuits and, more importantly, in their self-esteem and connection to community. I am sure the same is true for children like Emma and the many other children who each week play the instruments they're learning or perform songs with children's choirs for their church families. Some of these children may even grow to be the next choir directors who invite children to share their music in worship. The collective does as much to nurture confidence and skill in our children as parents do.

In the first-century Mediterranean world, individualism was practically unknown. Support from neighbors held communities together, both in times of joy and in times of mourning. The mourners who show up for the widow at Nain are a part of her and her son's community and so a part of their lives. Some may receive a small wage for the professional exercise of a duty, as mourning was treated in their culture, while others come and give of their time and resources to support a neighbor. Whether paid or not, each of them shows up not just to perform a ritual and move on but to offer support across all of this mother's aspects of need in that moment—ritual, social, emotional, and likely even material.

But here, too, the tragedy is amplified. It is not just a mother who has lost her son and the promise of the man he would grow to be; it is also a community who has lost a brother. The presence of the mourners suggests that this young man and his mother were, not unexpectedly, woven into the very fabric of their community. They were supported by and offered supports to their neighbors and community members. They knew and were known by one another. And now from this tapestry of community the boy's thread has been cut too soon. The communal support of the crowd around the woman both reassures her that she is not alone and amplifies the loss beyond her personal experience.

Only after having set up the circumstances of need and loss in this way does Luke narrate Jesus' interjection into this family's story. With a rapid series of verbs, Luke tells us, "When the Lord *saw* her, he *had compassion* for her and *said* to her, 'Do not weep.' Then he *came forward and touched* the bier" (7:13–14, emphasis added). There is no long conversation about what is going on. Jesus recognizes it immediately—interestingly, not in the funeral bier itself but in the grieving mother. Perhaps he sees the loss and need in the depths of her tear-stained eyes. Jesus asks neither the mother nor the mourners to explain themselves; he doesn't pause to take a moral inventory of the young man's life or ponder whether the young man deserves his compassion. Jesus is simply and radically moved by compassion. And so he acts.

Jesus' action freezes the procession in place. Immediately those carrying the funeral bier stand still (7:14). This shouldn't be assumed. People walk through crowded streets daily hearing calls for them to pause, and yet they move forward anyway, focused upon their task and unwilling to be deterred. In the midst of a funeral procession others may have greeted them on the road, perhaps even stepped forward to offer respects to the young man they were carrying or simply to determine the identity of the boy. But the procession must go forward. The bearers cannot be expected to stop for every stranger on the road.

And yet saying nothing to those holding the bier, Jesus simply steps forward. The bearers freeze. Do they recognize Jesus? It's possible that they have heard stories about Jesus and the miraculous works of healing he had done. Or maybe they are curious about the large crowd of disciples and other people who are following Jesus. Perhaps they don't know quite who he is but suspect he may be someone important. In any case, Jesus steps forward and the bearers freeze. What had been an ordinary, if tragic, funeral procession has now become unusual.

Soon, though, the procession takes a decidedly different turn. Jesus' initial words to the mother, "Do not weep," may have been perceived as insensitive or culturally out of place—it was her motherly duty to weep—but they weren't crazy talk. Perhaps his words may have been misconstrued as a poor attempt at consoling the mourning woman. However, with Jesus' next words, I have to imagine more than a few eyebrows were raised. Jesus says to the boy, "Young man, I say to you, rise!" (7:14). It's the same thing he said to the man with paralysis whom he healed in Capernaum (5:23), only this time the person on the stretcher whom Jesus addresses isn't merely paralyzed. He is dead.

If those who observed the healing miracle questioned Jesus' power or intent, surely those watching on this street in Nain might have wondered what Jesus had in mind. Was he simply confused? Did he not see the mourners? Did he not realize that the boy was not injured but dead? Was he trying to be funny? Surely this would have been ridiculed as a strange and insensitive kind of gallows humor, especially from an outsider entering the community. First, Jesus commands a widow and mourning mother not to weep, then he addresses a dead body and commands "rise!"

And yet while those in Nain may have been confused, those of us familiar with Luke's Gospel know what is to come. The Greek word translated "rise" (*egertheti*) that Jesus addresses to the boy on the bier comes from the same root as the word Jesus will later use to command Jairus's daughter, "Child, get up!" (8:54); to proclaim that the dead have been raised (7:22); and to speak of his own resurrection "on the third day" (9:22). Jesus isn't confused, and he isn't kidding around. Jesus and his followers may be traveling through Nain from another community, but in a larger sense, they—together with the boy, his mother, and the mourners who surround them—are part of an interdependent community; they are children of God looking forward to a brighter future. And as Jesus will soon have John's disciples relay, that future begins now.

In connection with a mother and her community, Jesus here takes another step forward into the inbreaking realm of God. At his bidding, "the blind receive their sight, the lame walk, the lepers are cleansed, the deaf hear, *the dead are raised*, the poor have good news brought to them" (7:22, emphasis added). What Jesus does for this family he doesn't do for his own sake. He doesn't even raise the boy on the funeral bier to prove God's power. Jesus acts for the sake of the young man and his family, small though it may be. He commands the mother to be calm and the boy to stand because *he has compassion for them*. Both of them.

In response the boy stands, resuscitated, and begins to speak. Jesus returns him to his mother. And Luke says of those present that "fear seized them all" and "they glorified God" (7:16). *All* is a big word. Presumably, this reaction spread not only through those carrying the funeral bier, the mourners, and those accompanying them, but also through mother, son, and the crowds accompanying Jesus. In their own way, they all reacted with a combination of inhibition and joy at the miraculous intervention in this pair's journey; at the same time, each reacted with and to one another. This is the power of community. It is the power of an act taken by one for the sake of another, in the presence of community, to effect change larger than itself.

Children in the Story

The Bearers of the Funeral Bier

At some level, adults know that children are present in ordinary life. When heading out to run errands, whether at a post office or a grocery store, few adults would honestly say that they *don't* expect to encounter any children along their way. At the same time, with the exception of visits to contemporary spaces specifically dedicated to children—such as playgrounds, schools, or children's museums—many adults rarely *think* about the presence of children. As we have seen in previous chapters, the same can be true about adult awareness of children's presence in worship. I wonder, for example, how much (if any) attention the other adults had paid to young Reagan in that evening worship service until Alene amplified her voice.

In the first-century Mediterranean world, few to no spaces were specifically dedicated to children. At the same time, the need to maintain the population despite high child mortality led to higher birth rates, resulting in nearly twice as many young children as adults in the population. Consequently, when one walked through a busy street, it would have felt like children were nearly everywhere. This wasn't due to any ideological commitment or particular affinity for children; it was simply the reality of the world in which Jesus lived.

By now I hope that you've begun to notice the presence of children in some of these assumed, ordinary spaces in the Gospel accounts where they might otherwise have been overlooked. As Jesus and his followers were walking along the road to Nain, there likely would have been children walking along that same road. Perhaps some particularly young children had ventured just a small way from home to gather water. Older children may have been on their way to the market. Others may have been on their way to a job or to visit a friend. There also would have been children among Jesus' followers, traveling with him on the road.

It doesn't take much imagination to picture children among the mourners following the widowed mother. Children could not have been shielded from the ever-present reality of death in their world. While children may not make up the majority of the attendees at contemporary funerals, many families bring their children to such services to pay respects to departed loved ones. Children may not now, nor perhaps in Jesus' time, fully understand death or the grief and loss entailed in it, but they are keen observers of their surroundings and their communities and so know something of grief and loss, even at an early age.

So it shouldn't come as a surprise that the "large crowd" (7:11) and the funeral procession would have involved children. Some of these children may have been looking on from afar, curious about the procession. Some may have been brought with their parents, even infants in arms. Perhaps they were confused by their parents' emotions, or anxious for the slow procession to come to a conclusion so that they could resume their ordinary activities. Others may have known the boy on the funeral bier personally. They may have been wrestling with their own sense of loss and mortality. They may have been missing a playmate, coworker, relative, or friend. In their own way, the children and adults in this intergenerational group certainly would have been mourning together.

But the children may not have been only at the sidelines of the crowds or at the outskirts of their mothers' garments. Evidence suggests that, at least sometimes, children and youth themselves participated in the ritual of funeral processions. Such life passages may, in fact, have highlighted a shared mortality that cut across generational divides. Especially in the case of a young person, it's likely that some who were closely connected to the newly deceased, in the same age group, would have wanted to help honor their friend. So while Luke doesn't give us detail one way or the other, it seems quite conceivable that at least some of those carrying this youth out of Nain would have themselves been children or youth—perhaps, like the deceased, boys on the cusp of adulthood. Maybe it is even the naiveté of such an age, the lack of experience in participating in this way in many funeral processions, that causes the bearers to stop so swiftly when Jesus steps forward into the road.

In any case, whether as bier bearers or as mourners in the crowd, children and young people participate in this boy's burial. These children, then, bear witness to Jesus' miraculous actions for one of their own. They see Jesus step forward and dare to touch the funeral bier that belongs not to an important state official or religious leader but a simple youth (7:14). The inclusiveness demonstrated by the attention that Jesus gives to this youth—the lowly son of a widow—would therefore not be lost on them.

When Jesus subsequently returns the youth to the home and care of his mother, the comfort and security so crucial to children, particularly at a young age, would thus be connected in their minds in a real and tangible way with Jesus' announcements of the advent of God's realm. Through the resuscitation of the youth at Nain, children in the crowds and among Jesus' followers experience the inclusive and secure invitation to the realm of God—extended to all of God's children.

The Resurrected Youth

In English translation, this story does not appear to involve any children. However, this is as much a result of the fact that most translators (and readers) of the Bible tend to assume the presence of adults when age is unspecified than it is of anything directly in the text. The first time that the widow's son is mentioned, the original text simply describes him as "the one who had died," without mentioning any age, even though most translations insert the word "man" (7:12, 15). Luke seems less concerned with the son's age than with the fact of his death. Only Jesus, perhaps because he does not view the son's death with the same finality, identifies him differently. Jesus calls the widow's son "young man."

Across continents and between the first and twenty-first centuries, the social expectations associated with youth have changed drastically. Nevertheless, certain physical manifestations remain constant, including the association of youthfulness with energy and vigor. The contrast between the narrator's reference to the widow's son as "one who had died" and Jesus' reference to him as a vivacious "youth" is striking. Jesus' call for this youth to return from the dead entails a return to the active and lively existence that his premature death had cut short. By publicly naming the young age of the person on the funeral bier, Jesus returns the widow's son to the boyish vitality that had been lost to him.

This link between youthfulness and resurrection is common to several biblical accounts. The Gospels only record Jesus raising two other people from the dead: Lazarus, the brother of Martha and Mary, who is of an unknown age (John 11:1–44; here again the term translated "certain man" is more literally "certain person"), and the daughter of Jairus, who is twelve years old (Luke 8:40–56) and so a youth herself. Similarly, in the Hebrew Bible the prophets Elijah and Elisha are each described as raising a young person from the dead (1 Kgs. 17:17–24; 2 Kgs. 4:18–37). This trope would not have been entirely unexpected. In the neighboring non-Jewish cultures of the ancient Near East and first-century Mediterranean, such resuscitations were understood as easier to achieve in young people because of the strength of their life force; hence, they were more common in practice and story.

In each of these stories—significantly, even in the ambiguous case of Lazarus—the person who is healed still resides in the family home. Multigenerational household relationships were more common in the ancient world than they are in the United States today, and so this does not mean that each of those characters must be read as a child. However, the overall pattern illustrates the interdependence between each of the people raised from the dead and the families to whom they return. The boys in the Hebrew Bible resurrection stories are the youngest in the group, likely in the middle to latter stages of childhood. At this age, the boys whom Elijah and Elisha raised would have been capable, when living, of speaking and acting for themselves in many ways. Yet they still required a significant amount of protection and provision from their families, as illustrated by the integral role of their mothers in these narratives.

On the other end of the spectrum, Lazarus is probably the eldest among those resurrected. John does not mention either parents or a spouse in relation to Lazarus, describing his unmarried sisters as arranging for his care. Although there is not enough information to know for sure, this seems to suggest that Lazarus and one or more of his sisters may be orphaned children. If we imagine that Mary and Martha are the same sisters from Luke's account (Luke 10:38–42), then it's possible that Martha is the eldest in the sibling group and so was left responsible for Mary and Lazarus, her two younger siblings.[2] On the other hand, if the two accounts refer to entirely different families, it is equally plausible that Lazarus is a young man, past the cusp of adulthood but not yet married. The widow's son and Jairus's daughter, then, fall just in the middle of these two extremes. The text describes both of them as youth who have either just reached or are not quite at the age of marriage.

As such, these young people before their deaths would have been learning their respective adult roles while still relying on the supports of their parents' household to sustain and strengthen them. This stage of young adulthood in the ancient world represented a delicate balance between continued dependence in certain areas, even as youth took on more responsibilities for themselves. This is a shift from practice to mastery and is not an instantaneous shift; rather, it involves a thousand different stops along the journey. The beginnings of such responsibility, for example, were being put into practice by Reagan when she agreed to help teach her classmates the Lord's Prayer. Or, returning to the music analogy, this transition may be seen at the moment in which a child's instrumental or vocal performance in worship shifts from being primarily a growth opportunity provided by the congregation for the sake of the child to a musical offering provided by the child for the sake of the community. While the gifts that children bring to community can always in some capacity enrich the whole, there comes a point when the gifts that they bring as they grow increase in depth and impact. For the widow's son, at this stage in his life, he was most likely learning the tools of his deceased father's trade and entering into civic relationships, while still depending, at least to a certain degree, upon his mother's resources and social connections to find his place. In the same way Reagan, confident as she was in her memorization, benefited from the support of her grandmother and Alene.

From Luke's text, we know that the widow's son continues to reside in his mother's home. This is indicated both by the lack of mention of any other family (wife or children), the presence of whom would have mitigated the tragedy of his widowed mother being left fully alone, as well as by the action of Jesus placing him, once resuscitated, back into his mother's care rather than the care of his own son or wife (7:15). From the cultural context, we know that by residing within his mother's home he would also have relied, at least in some ways, upon his mother's provisions. This is distinct from many adult-centered readings of the text that assume it is the widowed mother who needs her son and not the other way around. Prior to his death, surely, and now even more, in the state of vulnerability that his death and preceding illness or injury must have caused, the widow's son needs his mother.

This is not to say that the mother did not need her son. Most families in the first century lived very near the poverty line and relied upon the work of each member of the family in order to survive. In such a small family as the one that Luke here describes, mother and son would have relied upon one another. Especially since the son is in the vital stage of youth that reflects an increase in strength and ability, his labor would likely have been essential to his mother, just as the security that his mother provided would have been essential to him.

Here it is important to note that the state of widowhood in the first century, while not ideal, was not as dire as some commentators make it out to have been. Within limits, women were able to maintain property and, for wealthy women, even substantial influence after their husbands' deaths. In fact, for a woman with enough means not to rely upon her husband's labor, widowhood could actually increase certain liberties and influence. Without knowing much about the social or economic status of the widow of Nain, it would be too much to assume that she was financially stable without her son; however, her son's presence alone would not have been the key to achieving her sustainability. At the same time, after the death of his father, whatever social or financial stability the son had a hope of receiving would have come from the household maintained and bequeathed by his widowed mother as the boy matured. In this state, both mother and son rely upon one another for survival. It is not that either one would be unable to survive without the other, but that it would be that much more of a struggle. Instead, they rely upon one another as partners.

But survival is not all that is at stake in this story. This is also a story of loss and grieving—for the boy, the loss of life; for his mother, the loss of her son. Luke does not explain the mother's grief except to say that her son has died. Although concern about her survival in his absence may have been a part of her grief, both text and context suggest that it is not the whole story. Funeral processions were a typical part of first-century Jewish mourning for all but the youngest of children and typically involved both family and community members as well as paid wailers. The larger mourning ritual also required that the household refrain from working during the period of mourning. The very fact that the mother is holding a funeral procession, which would have come at some cost to her, suggests that her grief is not solely economic.

A plain-sense understanding of grief at the loss of a family member that this mother holds dear seems to be assumed. Although high infant mortality rates in the ancient world made it difficult to fully mourn each young child lost to a family, deaths past early childhood were significantly less common. For this reason, historian of ancient Rome Suzanne Dixon describes the most "tragic or untimely death" in this time period to have been that of a young person in just the age range as Jesus places the widow's son—a child "who had survived long enough for parents to form expectations that the child would outlive them."[3] In other words, a mother of such a youthful son would mourn the loss of her child, and with him the hopes and dreams that she had begun to attach to him. Here we begin to see a different kind of dependency; the mother is dependent upon her son for the fulfillment of their family's future, just as the young man remains dependent upon his mother in order to reach that future goal.

It is within the interconnected relationship between mother and son that Luke's narrative begins. Following upon the young man's death, a crowd attends his mother. Amid this scene, brought about by the son, Jesus then notices the mother. A reading of this text that focuses solely or even primarily upon the mother and her needs runs the risk of seeing the son only as a means to the mother's ends, thus missing the interconnected relationship between mother and son. It is impossible to see the mother as the grieving mother she is without also seeing the son. Once we recognize this, it is not difficult to read beyond the details of the text to notice the extent of Jesus' compassion. As we see in the various accounts of Jesus feeding the crowds, compassion is not something that Jesus possesses in limited supply (see Mark 6:34). Jesus' compassion is first directed to the grieving mother (7:13), but his speech and actions from that point indicate that he is also drawn in, through her, to the needs of her son.

Were Jesus' concern only for the widow—whether due to her social, economic, or even emotional state—there would have been any number of other ways to resolve her troubles without any attention to her son. Jesus could have called the dead youth's mother to join with him, where she would later be cared for in the fellowship of believers (Acts 2:44–45) and by the community's provision for widows (cf. Luke 20:46–47; Acts 6:1–6). He might have helped to arrange a new marriage for her, placed her in the care of a prominent member of the community, or connected her with a new adopted son (as he does for his own mother at the cross in John 19:26–27). A move by Jesus to incorporate the widow in some way into his growing discipleship circle would have been even more reflective of Luke's concern and value for widows. From an economic standpoint, such focused attention on the widow would have resulted in more immediate returns for her. Instead, Jesus returns to her a boy who remains dependent upon her for his own needs as much, if not more, than she is dependent upon him. In so doing, Jesus may alleviate some of the widow's economic woes, but if that were his only concern, it is a highly inefficient way of addressing it.

Instead of taking any of these hypothetical expedients, Jesus, concerned not only with the widow, returns to her a youthful son—a boy not yet married, not yet the head of his own home, and not yet financially independent. In other words, his actions, while magnanimous, are not entirely practical. The resurrection of the boy does not seem to be the simplest or even most certain solution to the sort of financial or social problems that the widow might face. By raising the boy, Jesus does not even guarantee that he will not die again and thus leave her in much the same position as before. However, as an act of compassion, Jesus reunites mother and son. He does not solve all of their problems, but he restores their *relationship*. The once-grieving mother has, once again, a hope for the future and, of course, the precious life of her son. Likewise, the once-deceased child shares in the hopes and the joys of his mother when Jesus returns him to her.

Luke tells us that after healing the boy, Jesus "gave him" to his mother (7:15). In connection with a mother-son relationship, this action is less about bestowing an object so much as it is about delivering a person into the care of another; in short, Jesus entrusts the young man to his mother. The son is not the mother's rightful possession whom Jesus *returns*; rather, this youth, restored to life, is a precious child of God with whose care Jesus *entrusts* his mother.[4]

The relationship is two-sided. While acknowledging the unhappy reality that many parents in Roman antiquity, like this widow, found themselves prematurely burying their children, Dixon explains the prevailing cultural hopes and expectations of the day in terms of *pietas*, a Latin word for piety or duty, which "laid down certain claims within the family which ideally governed relations between the generations."[5]

The individuals in a family, even one as small as two persons, were dependent upon each other. The son was expected to care for the mother, just as the mother was expected to care for him.

In this story lies much more than the typical return to fortune that traditional interpretations would point us to. A childist interpretation allows us to see the much deeper, restorative power of relationship in Jesus' recognition of *both* mother *and* son. Jesus' compassion extends to both individuals because only when mother and son are reunited is the healing of either one of them complete.

The strength of their bond may also be imagined in the space between the youth's speech and Jesus' action. Although Luke does not report what the youth says, the text is clear that the youth does speak. It is then left to us as readers to fill in the gap of what the youth says. If our only attention is on the needs and concerns of the widow, we may miss the opportunity. However, when we acknowledge the youth as an active participant in the mother-son relationship, then what he says begins to take on a new importance. After all, a lively and vivacious youth, once restored to life, likely would not allow himself to be a pawn of either Jesus or his mother. What he speaks, then, must have some influence on the action that follows. It is possible that in keeping with Luke's concern that resurrections be corroborated by the physical act of eating, the young man may have asked in his first words for something to eat (cf. Luke 8:55; 24:40–41). Alternately, he may have expressed confusion, or perhaps even thanks to Jesus. But if the next act has anything to do with what the youth may have said, it is equally possible, and perhaps even more probable, that the young man's first words were to ask for his mother.

Such a response seems consistent with the timeless impulse of a scared or injured child—even a teenager—calling out for a trusted caregiver, who brings security and peace. Moreover, if this is the content of the boy's speech, then it transforms our reading of what may otherwise seem an abrupt movement of Jesus' attention away from the child and toward the mother into a tender acknowledgment of the bond between them. Such a progression affirms that one cannot give attention to one member of this pairing without also acknowledging the other. The compassion that Jesus extends encompasses both mother and son and, through their relationship, restores and intensifies hope both in their family and their community.

Cocreation in Relationship

It's commonly said that "practice makes perfect"; however, in relationships perfection isn't an attainable or perhaps even desirable goal. One of my daughter's first violin teachers used to frequently remind us, "Practice doesn't make *perfect*. Practice makes *permanent*." This is why it's so hard for us to relearn familiar texts like the Lord's Prayer or to recite favorite Bible passages in a different translation. From frequent repetition over long periods of times, these words are no longer simply memorized—they have become a part of us.

The message is clear—strive to correct mistakes, rather than perpetuating them, to avoid solidifying bad habits. However, when we solidify *good* habits, the rewards are bountiful. We take the fruits of such practice for granted on a regular basis. For example, we rarely think about the practice involved when we appreciate the ease with which our church organist plays a well-known hymn; when those gathered in worship repeat standard prayers, praise choruses, and more; or when a child maintains a steady pace on a bicycle. The beauty of practice is that when done right, it makes a task with which we might have once struggled suddenly appear easy. Indeed, it may even transform the same task into something fun.

The same is true of relationships. Paul writes to the young church leader Timothy about living in relationship within the body of Christ:

> Let no one despise your youth, but set the believers an example in speech and conduct, in love, in faith, in purity. Until I arrive, give attention to the public reading of scripture, to exhorting, to teaching. Do not neglect the gift that is in you, which was given to you through prophecy with the laying on of hands by the council of elders. Put these things into practice, devote yourself to them, so that all may see your progress. Pay close attention to yourself and to your teaching; continue in these things, for in doing this you will save both yourself and your hearers. (1 Tim. 4:12–16)

What Paul is describing is a process of cocreation, of leader and assembly coming into being and creating a new thing through their trust and engagement with one another. It is the act of one dissonant voice drawing in, rather than pulling apart, the voice of the assembly.

Church families, of course, are not perfect, no more so than any family is. We may be tempted to despise or dismiss the perceived errors of others, especially of the youngest among us. However, Paul calls us instead to persist, to practice what it means to be faithful together, when necessary to correct our mistakes but also to strive for more joy than sorrow and more cooperation than rebuke, in hopes that it is these things that become our permanent way of being with and caring for one another. As members of the body of Christ, we must practice every day what it means to be members of one another.

At the same time, Paul knew all too well that such preparation is not always easy. When I was a teenager, I remember learning for the first time that the "sharing of the peace" that was a part of our worship liturgy has roots in Jesus' command to reconcile yourself to your brother or sister before coming to the altar (Matt. 5:23–24). This was a particularly hard pill to swallow on Sundays when I had quarreled with my family before coming to church. However, as I lived into it, what had previously just been shaking hands became for me a much more difficult, but meaningful, act of reconnection.

Now as an adult, at the seminary where I teach, we don't practice the sharing of the peace in that way in our regular chapel service, but in the form of a Black gospel song we sing regularly, Hezekiah Walker's "I Need You to Survive." Our music minister invites us to turn toward somebody sitting around us in worship and look them in the eye as we sing the powerful lyrics, which include these lines:

> I need you, you need me.
> We're all a part of God's body.
> . . . .
> I pray for you, You pray for me.
> I love you, I need you to survive.[6]

My experience in the "pull yourself up by your bootstraps" culture of White middle-class America has emphasized independence to a fault, which I continue to wrestle to overcome. This is not everyone's experience. Those who are a part of the African American community know too well that systemic and legal discrimination have not only deprived members of their community of the proverbial bootstraps but have pushed them back down when they manage to pull themselves up anyway. Black and Brown people across America, as well as people discriminated against due to the countries they were born in, the languages they speak, the gods they worship, or the physical and mental abilities they possess, know more deeply the fundamental human need we have for one another. These communities know this both because they have lived the harms of being deprived of communal support from the larger society and because they have lived the blessings of supporting and uplifting one another. Such knowledge is one of the many gifts that womanist theology brings to the church.

The difference between sharing God's peace independently, even with someone with whom I may need to be reconciled, and looking that same person in the eye and admitting that I need them is life altering. At one chapel service in which we sang this song, I was seated next to William, my seven-year-old son. I probably had much to reconcile with him that day, since we had been attempting to tolerate one another as he endured sitting in my office on a day off from school and I attempted to work despite his persistent interruptions. But when I looked into his eyes and declared my *need* for him, it was not simply or even primarily about getting through the day; I was reminded of his importance in my life, in my family, and in the shared body of Christ. I realized I didn't need him to behave; I just needed *him*. I need him, just as deeply as he needs me. This is the interplay that happens when we pray together—when the lines are blurred between who is praying with or for whom and, instead, we simply pray.

It is also, I think, what Jesus intends for the widow and her son when he gives the boy back to his mother. There isn't necessarily a sense of ownership here, as though the son is the mother's to possess or the mother is her son's to possess or command, nor is there a sense of unidirectional dependency, as though the woman cannot survive without her son or vice versa. Instead, there is a sense of community, of the multidirectional nature of the give-and-take between the faithful who depend upon one another. Such practice—such trust—is, indeed, how we care for and perhaps even save one another. It is how we grow and become our best selves together. For the mother and son in Nain, embracing this gift of interdependency means joining a community of selves that embody mutual support—the same community that showed up to support this young man in his death and his mother in her grief.

This is the push and pull that defines the hard work of creation, of becoming, that all relationships, but especially those between children and their caregivers, entail. It isn't easy to rely upon someone, and if I'm being honest with myself as a parent, it isn't always easy to be relied upon as fully as children, especially young children, rely upon their parents. However, such work is literally life-giving. In her survey of African American mothering and womanist maternal thought, Stephanie Buckhanon Crowder explains, "Womanist maternal thought defines work as an activity that brings wholeness and health to children. This work occurs in the home and outside its environs."[7] In whatever ways their individual, social, and cultural circumstances call for, mothers—and, Buckhanon adds, "other mothers" (like Alene) from one's family, community, and church—work daily at bringing wholeness for their children and, through them, their communities.

At the same time, as Paul reminds Timothy, young people can bring wholeness—even salvation—to their communities too. The gift of living in community is being able to recognize when you are needed and when you need someone else. In the culture in which I was raised, which heavily values independence, it takes work to practice interdependence. It takes work to let the imperfection of another human being into my space and life, to adjust my words or my practice for another. It's all too easy to leave questions unasked in a Bible study class out of a desire to not admit one doesn't know the answer, or to go hungry rather than accept a donation from a church food pantry in a time of need. But as Alene Bush modeled, when we come alongside those in our community who may not be the same as us but who share the same needs for encouragement and affirmation, there is much joy to be found. Indeed, when practicing such relationships long enough, it's possible that we might even come to realize that those for whom we make space in our lives have made space for us and our imperfections too.

Such interdependence is the supreme gift and joy of relationship. To be in relationship, to call oneself "mother" or "father" or call one's offspring "daughter" or "son" means to live into these tensions. It also means that when the relationship is challenged or strained, there is no simple or easy solution, no single problem to be solved. There is only the grief and joy of creating new bonds together. This is the challenge and the hope that Luke conveys in the story of mother and son at the gate of Nain. It is perhaps especially true as mother and son live into this relationship without any other immediate family members to support them.

In Luke's story, a young man is restored to life. However, perhaps more significantly, the relationship between a mother and a son is restored. Together, mother and son are returned to one another. From this account of healing and restoration, we witness the glory of God's grace extended to children and parents as well as the gift and promise of such relationships—especially in the creative partnerships of those who entrust themselves to one another.

Theologian Cristina Grenholm describes motherhood as "not merely about procreation" but "the coming into being of human beings in communion with others."[8] She doesn't mean by this that children aren't already fully human beings at birth. There isn't a magical age at which a child (or an adult) becomes human any more than there is a magical moment at which a person becomes a parent. Rather, we are all and always continually becoming. This means that as Christ's body, we must make space for one another to practice.

Church families would do well to pay attention to the various gifts and needs of those around them, especially youth and children still finding their way. It's worth noting that when Alene noticed the difference in Reagan's prayer, she could have responded differently. While it's unlikely (I hope) that any worshiper would outright taunt a child, another person might have ignored or corrected Reagan. While such actions may have led to a more uniform and "perfect" auditory effect, at best they would have missed an opportunity for a community to come together, and at worst potentially discouraged or disheartened a child who had, moments earlier, been enthusiastic about a faith milestone.

Unfortunately, churches and individuals frequently miss such opportunities to come alongside and affirm children, to everyone's detriment. This happens when children's art is set aside dismissively rather than displayed with pride of place in a worship or education space; when a congregation, many of whose youth play in the community's high school band, hires a professional brass quartet to play for Easter worship rather than approaching the students first; or when children or youth are passed over when a ministry leader is looking for someone to pray because they aren't "old" or "mature" enough. While there is little doubt that a member of the trumpet faculty at a nearby university will play the accompaniment for "Jesus Christ Is Risen Today" with more dynamics than a member of the congregation's youth group, there is value in weighing whose contribution will add more, overall, to the gifts of community in worship.

Rather than striving for perfection, the gift of community is to nurture the permanence of our relationships and connections with one another. When done well, it is possible that that same freshman trumpeter may one day return to his home congregation to play a beautiful descant on Easter. In the meantime, when we recognize the gifts and talents of those in our midst, we continue on the journey of becoming together.

This is why it's so important that we not talk about children as the "future" of the church, their country, or the world—or at least not solely so. Children are most certainly the future. Who they are and how they live into their communities will help to define what the church and the world will become. But children are also and just as importantly the present. Children are a part of the church, members of the same body, sharers with Christ in the unfolding mission of God's realm *now*. Children are already citizens of their community, nation, and this world from the very moment of their birth, even as they continue to grow into what all of this means as they age. Therefore, when we think about the role—or more accurately, roles—of children in the church, it is insufficient to imagine their participation in the future. Rather, it's necessary to practice together with children what it means to be the church today.

Recognizing this need to be together in a new way, Lutheran pastor Andrea Roske-Metcalfe went so far as to reenvision the worship space in the congregation she served to meet the needs of both children and adults, creating a "Pray-Ground" that, after unexpected news coverage, has become a national movement. The idea of a Pray-Ground is that everyone—adults and children—not only belong in worship together but deserve a space that allows them to participate fully. Similar ideas can and should be applied for disabled and nondisabled worshipers as well. In the case of adults and children, Roske-Metcalfe began by acknowledging that traditional pews and chairs, containing hymnals and Bibles, typically facilitate adult worship in her context well. She then asked what would do the same for children. The result was moving away one section of pews in the front of the church and replacing it with comfortable rugs, child-size tables and chairs, soft toys and books, and art supplies. Roske-Metcalfe was quoted in a 2016 article:

> I know how hard it is as a parent with kids to get out the door in the first place. I want families with young children to know once they get in the door that there's a place for them. . . . The [Pray-Ground] serves as a visual reminder every time we gather as church that kids aren't an afterthought. They are a vital part of the congregation.[9]

For the people at First Church, Alene affirmed this through prayer. At Good Shepherd, the contemporary worship leader, Deanna, signaled this vital connection in a different way. Whether in recruiting members of the worship praise band or inviting community members to read Scripture or share a prayer, she was always intentional about including people of all ages—children, teenagers, and adults—not just as participants, but as collaborators. Not only were children invited to read the prayers, but they were invited—together with their families—to help write the prayers. Not only were teens invited to sing in the band, but they were invited—and sometimes led the way—to help choose music that was relevant and interesting to them. At the same time, adults continued writing other prayers and selecting other music. In this way, the worship service and those who led it modeled a collaborative experience.

The parent-child relationship—and, indeed, the relationships among all those who nurture and are nurtured by another—is defined not by a moment of time but by a shared journey, by a need and willingness to define ourselves with and through one another. It doesn't demand the prioritization of one person or the other. Rather, it requires a *return* to one another, a slowing down, as Alene did, to recognize the needs of the other, even if that return involves reshaping or reenvisioning our words, practices, or physical space. Such sharing, cocreation as Grenholm calls it, is equal parts difficult and rewarding. I am apt to place the emphasis on one or the other depending upon which day you ask me (and I suspect my children would agree). This is not limited to parents and their children. It is a bond that transcends cultural definitions and demands only, as Paul asks, that as fellow human beings we be members of one another. And when we commit to such partnership, together our voices can join in the beautiful praise of God—regardless of the particular words or practices we employ.

In their restored relationship, the widow and her son model this kind of partnership. Through Jesus' gift of returning them to one another, they experience not only renewed life together but also mutual trust and security. Together they rely upon each other. Through Jesus' re-creation, mother and son are thus able to continue to create together. Indeed, as they glorify Jesus in this text, they have already begun to create something new.

The inclusive grace and welcome extended at Nain, therefore, moves beyond the experience of one mother or one son to encompass more broadly God's plan for the salvation of all of God's children through the life, death, and ministry of God's own son—Jesus. The healing of this youth is more than one moment of gratuitous inclusion. More important than this individual moment of miraculous accomplishment for Jesus, this experience highlights the personal nature of God's involvement with the world—giving individuals to one another in community, in discipleship, and, here at Nain, in family. The relational bond between mother and child is restored, and in its restoration they join together in creating the restorative vision that God has for the world.

For Further Reading

Dixon, Suzanne. *The Roman Mother*. Norman: Oklahoma University Press, 1989.

Grenholm, Cristina. *Motherhood and Love: Beyond Gendered Stereotypes of Theology*. Translated by Marie Tåqvist. Grand Rapids: Eerdmans, 2011.

Gumbs, Alexis Pauline, China Martens, and Mai'a Williams, eds. *Revolutionary Mothering: Love on the Front Lines.* Toronto: Between the Lines, 2016.

Kim-Cragg, KyeRae. *Interdependence: A Postcolonial Feminist Practical Theology*. Eugene, OR: Pickwick, 2018.

McWilliam, Janette. "The Socialization of Roman Children." In *The Oxford Handbook of Childhood and Education in the Classical World,* edited by Judith Grubbs, Tim Parkin, and Roslynne Bell. Oxford: Oxford University Press, 2013.

Questions for Discussion

1. In what ways do you think the mother in Luke's story needed her son? In what ways might the son also have needed his mother?
2. Describe a relationship in which you have felt the mutual interchange of cocreation (perhaps as a child, parent, partner, or friend). In what ways have you needed the other in this relationship? In what ways has the other person needed you?
3. Are interdependent relationships the norm, or are they anomalous in your cultural context? What are the greatest challenges posed by these sorts of interdependent relationships? What are the greatest blessings?
4. How has community nurtured your gifts and helped you to grow? Who are the "other mothers" (or "fathers") in your life who have encouraged you in this growth and partnered with you on the journey?
5. In what ways does living in relationship with other humans allow you to extend God's grace beyond those relationships? In what ways might this have happened for the widow and her son as well?

Conclusion

Ministry with Children as Gift and Calling

Over a decade ago, when I began my journey of parenting from the pews, I imagined that I had a wealth of spiritual insight to impart to my children. I shared a similar conceit about my entry into biblical studies at the same time, with the notion that I was preparing for a career of dispensing biblical knowledge to my students. In the intervening years, I cannot deny that I *have* grown in both spiritual and biblical wisdom, but more than this, I have grown into the understanding that knowledge and spirituality are best shared in mutual exploration rather than in hierarchical dispensation. As a result, my vision and expectation of who is ministering to whom and what that ministry is really about have shifted as well.

Since I relocated my participation in the Sunday morning liturgy to the pews, our family has continued to be blessed by the presence of gracious faith mentors in many of the church families in which my children and I have worshiped, the stories of each too numerous to count. However, even more than the ministry of our extended church families, I have come to know the gift of ministry imparted by my children *themselves*. Even as I hoped to teach them about what it meant to be a part of God's family, my children have succeeded far more successfully in teaching me just that.

Not long after I traded my place at the altar for the pew, the scribbles that our daughter Becca was intent to make on bulletins, scrap paper, and anything she could find began to take on more discernible shapes. One of the first shapes that Becca learned to draw was the cross. This was probably due in no small part to two things: first, most of her drawing skills developed while she was doodling on a small clipboard kept in the cloth "church bags" at the church we attended; second, at the very center of that same church, a large and impressive wooden cross hung from the ceiling. Becca associated this cross with God's love and enjoyed producing multiple copies of her artwork and distributing them to those who sat near us during the sharing of the peace.

Several years later I had the privilege of accompanying our second child, Joanna, to the altar as she received her First Communion—an experience no less meaningful for me than when I, as pastor, had placed the first taste of that same meal in her sister's hands. Since Joanna was born, whenever the bread and the cup were lifted at the altar, I would point this moment out and quietly exclaim, "Look! There's Jesus!" At one year old, as Joanna began to develop an awareness of the people around her, this led to some confusion, and one day she pointed to a picture of the senior pastor of that congregation on a wall and crowed excitedly, "Jesus!" But soon after the confusion was cleared away, she was eager to receive Jesus in the bread and the wine. However, whatever message I thought I was getting through to her was quickly replaced with the message she imparted to me when, after receiving the meal, I asked my boisterous one-year-old where Jesus was and she pointed meaningfully at her belly and then her heart, replying, "Here!" Jesus comes to us, enters into us, and whatever the sermon that Sunday may have been, the gospel was made plain to me in that moment with Joanna.

But perhaps the greatest reminder of God's work in and through children has come from our youngest child. By no fault of his own, William's early experiences in worship were quite mixed. At six years old, he had shifted between congregations that were completely and unabashedly welcoming, and those that have put up walls and barriers for children in their midst. As a result, somewhere along the way, I became less pointed in my approach. I allowed William to read rather than sing along with every song, as I coaxed his sisters to do. Sometimes I forgot, or just didn't bother, to point out when the elements of Communion were lifted up. I lapsed in reciting the Lord's

Prayer to him by rote when he was a young toddler. Yet William began to pick up the words to the Lord's Prayer himself, from continuous exposure more than anything else. Around the same time, this little man threw me completely for a loop when, one day, he picked up his children's Bible and began to read, moving from cover to cover in a matter of days. As he read, he paused to ask questions, make comments, and engage me in familiar stories that, despite my livelihood as a biblical scholar, brought the text to life for me in entirely new ways.

Not every child in worship is the same, any more than that could be said of every adult. The interest levels and points of engagement for each person are different. I do not believe it was coincidental that Jesus called *fishers* to *fish* for people any more so than that he affirmed both Mary and Martha in their different but important responses. The young boy who brought the fish and loaves to Jesus was no more or less a disciple than the men who distributed them. The point is not what we do as we participate in Christian ministry, but *that* we participate together. As Paul writes, "For as in one body we have many members, and all the members do not have the same function, so we, though many, are one body in Christ, and individually members one of another" (Rom. 12:4–5).

By exploring anew familiar stories with the roles and questions of children at the center, my hope is that your understanding of Christ's body has broadened to see the place of children not as future appendages of an institution we love, but rather as precious and irreplaceable members with us in a mission we share. Just as the shepherds received both gift and calling on that hill outside Bethlehem, so we, both adults and children, are called both to minister to and for one another as we hasten the coming realm of God—a realm that Jesus promises belongs to none other than these little ones in our midst.

Notes

Foreword

1. Marty Haugen, "Let Us Build a House (All Are Welcome)," in *Glory to God* (Louisville, KY: Westminster John Knox Press, 2013), #301.

Introduction

1. These strategies are laid out as the pillars of childist interpretation in the introduction and conclusion of *Children and Methods: Listening to and Learning from Children in the Biblical World*, ed. Kristine Henriksen Garroway and John W. Martens (Leiden: Brill, 2020).

Chapter 1: The Gift of Participation

1. In Matthew's Gospel account, the scene is set differently and leads to Jesus' disciples directly asking him, "Who is the greatest in the kingdom of heaven?" (18:1).
2. For a history of origin and reception of this song, see Harry Eskew, "From Civil War Song to Children's Hymn: 'Jesus Loves the Little Children,'" in *We'll Shout and Sing Hosanna: Essays on Church Music in Honor of William J. Reynolds*, ed. David W. Music (Fort Worth: School of Church Music, Southwestern Theological Seminary, 1998), 262.
3. Eunyung Lim, *Entering God's Kingdom (Not) Like a Little Child: Images of the Child in Matthew, 1 Corinthians, and Thomas* (Berlin: De Gruyter, 2021), 59–60.
4. Bonnie Miller-McLemore, "Jesus Loves the Little Children? An Exercise in the Use of Scripture," *Journal of Childhood and Religion* 1 (2010): 22.
5. For more on early Jewish blessings of children, see Judith M. Gundry, "Children in the Gospel of Mark, with Special Attention to Jesus' Blessing of the Children (Mark 10:13–16) and the Purpose of Mark," in *The Child in the Bible*,

ed. Marcia Bunge, Terence E. Fretheim, and Beverly Roberts Gaventa (Grand Rapids: Eerdmans, 2008), 155.

Chapter 2: The Gift of Proclamation

1. Tim Parkin, "Demography of Infancy and Early Childhood," in *The Oxford Handbook of Childhood and Education in the Classical World*, ed. Judith Evans Grubbs, Tim Parkin, and Roslynne Bell (Oxford: Oxford University Press, 2013), 43–44.
2. Parkin, 48.
3. Mitzi J. Smith, "Abolitionist Messiah: A Man Named Jesus Born of a Doule," in *Bitter the Chastening Rod: Africana Biblical Interpretation after* Stony the Road We Trod *in the Age of BLM, SayHerName, and MeToo*, ed. Mitzi J. Smith, Angela N. Parker, and Ericka S. Dunbar Hill (Lanham, MD: Lexington/Fortress, 2022), 54.
4. Smith, 55, citing Clarice J. Martin, "Womanist Interpretations of the New Testament: The Quest for Holisitc and Inclusive Translation and Interpretation," in *I Found God in Me: A Womanist Biblical Hermeneutics Reader* (Eugene, OR: Cascade, 2015), 25.
5. Smith, 60.
6. "The Room of the Slaves—The Latest Discovery at Civita Giuliana," *Pompeii*, November 6, 2021, http://pompeiisites.org/en/comunicati/the-room-of-the-slaves-the-latest-discovery-at-civita-giuliana/.
7. Wilda C. Gafney, *Womanist Midrash: A Reintroduction to Women of the Torah and the Throne* (Louisville, KY: Westminster John Knox Press, 2017), 55.
8. PT Kid 1.7, quoted in Hagith Sivan, *Jewish Childhood in the Roman World* (Cambridge: Cambridge University Press, 2018), 106.
9. T Hag 1.3–4, quoted in Sivan, 113.
10. If we understand Mary as an enslaved virgin, Smith argues in contrast that "Mary must have been quite young," since enslaved women were often "penetrated against their will at an early age" (Smith, "Abolitionist Messiah," 59).
11. Richard W. Voelz, *Youthful Preaching* (Eugene, OR: Cascade, 2016), 9.

Chapter 3: The Gift of Advocacy

1. The designation "the Twelve" occurs repeatedly throughout the Gospel accounts and the beginning of Acts, especially in the crucifixion narratives: Matt. 10:2; 19:28; 20:17; 26:14, 20, 47; Mark 3:16; 4:10; 6:7; 9:35; 10:32; 11:11; 14:10, 17, 20, 43; Luke 8:1; 9:1, 12; 18:31; 22:3, 30, 47; John 6:67, 70; 20:24; Acts 6:2; and 7:8.
2. Where the Synoptics have Bartholomew, John replaces him with Nathaniel (John 1:45–49; 21:2); the tax collector, Matthew in the Gospel account so named, is called Levi by Mark and Luke (Mark 2:14; Luke 5:27); and where Matthew and Mark read Thaddeus, Luke and John read a second Judas (Luke 6:16; John 14:22).

3. Luke refers to the Sea of Galilee as "Lake Gennesaret" (Luke 5:1), which is the same body of water known as Lake Kinneret or Lake Tiberias today. To avoid confusion, I refer to this body of water as the Sea of Galilee throughout, since this is how it is most frequently referred to throughout the New Testament.
4. Aelian, *On the Nature of Animals,* 15.5.

Chapter 4: The Gift of Listening

1. In each instance in Luke and Acts where someone is described as learning at the foot of another, it is possible if not certain that these persons are still children. This is the case for Jesus and the elders (Luke 2:46), Paul and Gamaliel (Acts 22:3), and here, Mary and Jesus.
2. Paulo Freire, *Pedagogy of the Oppressed*, trans. Myra Bergman (New York: Continuum, 1970), 71.
3. Tex Sample, *Ministry in an Oral Culture: Living with Will Rogers, Uncle Remus, and Minnie Pearl* (Louisville, KY: Westminster John Knox, 1994), 14.
4. Richard Shaull, "Foreword to the Original English Edition (1970)," in *Pedagogy of the Oppressed: 50th Anniversary Edition*, by Paulo Freire, 4th ed. (Bloomsbury: Bloomsbury Academic, 2015), 219.

Chapter 5: The Gift of Sharing

1. The Greek word translated "these people" here is actually a demonstrative pronoun meaning "these" that refers back to the crowd.
2. Susan P. Mattern, *The Prince of Medicine: Galen in the Roman Empire* (Oxford: Oxford University Press, 2013), 184; see also Sharon Betsworth, "John," in *Children in Early Christian Narratives* (London: Bloomsbury T&T Clark, 2015), 138.
3. See, for example, Marianne Bjelland Kartzow, "Slave Children in the Jesus Movement," in *Childhood in History: Perceptions of Children in the Ancient and Medieval Worlds*, ed. Reidar Aasgaard and Cornelia Horn, with Oana Maria Cojocaru (London: Routledge, 2018), 115; Jennifer A. Glancy, *Slavery in Early Christianity* (Oxford: Oxford University Press, 2002), 92–101; and Emerson B. Powery, "Reading with the Enslaved: Placing Human Bondage at the Center of the Early Christian Story," in *Bitter the Chastening Rod: Africana Biblical Interpretation after* Stony the Road We Trod *in the Age of BLM and SayHerName and MeToo*, ed. Mitzi J. Smith, Angela N. Parker, and Ericka Dunbar Hill (Lanham, MD: Lexington/Fortress, 2022), 72.
4. For the connection between these two stories, see Betsworth, "John," 140–141. It must be noted, however, that fish were relatively common in peasant diets of the time, especially along the Sea of Galilee, regardless of vocation.
5. Betsworth, 139.
6. Shively T. J. Smith, *Strangers to Family: Diaspora and 1 Peter's Invention of God's Household* (Waco: Baylor University Press, 2016), 19.

Chapter 6: The Gift of Partnership

1. See chapter 2, notes 1 and 2.
2. See chapter 3 on the age and status of Mary and Martha in their household. According to Roman and Jewish law, Martha would not have inherited her family's property if she had a brother. However, if her brother was not yet an adult, she may have served as custodian over their household until Lazarus came of age.
3. Suzanne Dixon, *The Roman Mother* (Norman: Oklahoma University Press, 1989), 100.
4. This same relationship can be seen in Jesus' teachings about stewardship in Luke. See, for example, the parable of the nobleman who entrusts his money to his stewards while he is away (Luke 19:13–15; cf. 12:48).
5. Suzanne Dixon, *The Roman Family* (Baltimore: Johns Hopkins University Press, 1992), 157.
6. Lyrics.com, STANDS4 LLC, 2023. "I Need You to Survive Lyrics," https://www.lyrics.com/lyric/5731963/Hezekiah+Walker/I+Need+You+To+Survive.
7. Stephanie Buckhanon Crowder, *When Momma Speaks: The Bible and Motherhood from a Womanist Perspective* (Louisville, KY: Westminster John Knox, 2016), 23.
8. Cristina Grenholm, *Motherhood and Love: Beyond the Gendered Stereotypes of Theology*, trans. Marie Tåqvist (Grand Rapids: Eerdmanns, 2011), 31.
9. Erin Strybis, "See How Children Experience Church through This 'Pray-Ground,'" *Living Lutheran*, June 7, 2016.